Microsoft®

SharePoint® 2010 Plain & Simple

Johnathan Lightfoot and Chris Beckett

Published with the authorization of Microsoft Corporation by:
O'Reilly Media, Inc.
1005 Gravenstein Highway North
Sebastopol, California 95472

Printed and bound in Canada.

4 5 6 7 8 9 10 11 12 TI 6 5 4 3 2 1

Microsoft Press titles may be purchased for educational, business or sales promotional use. Online editions are also available for most titles (*http://my.safaribooksonline.com*). For more information, contact our corporate/institutional sales department: (800) 998-9938 or *corporate@ oreilly.com*. Visit our website at *microsoftpress.oreilly.com*. Send comments to *mspinput@microsoft.com*.

Acquisitions and Developmental Editor: Kenyon Brown
Production Editor: Rachel Monaghan
Copy Editor: John Pierce
Editorial Production: Octal Publishing, Inc.
Technical Reviewer: Troy Lanphier
Indexer: Ron Strauss
Compositors: Ron Bilodeau and Nellie McKesson
Illustrator: Robert Romano

This book uses Otabind™, a durable and flexible lay-flat binding.

978-0-735-64228-7   [2011-12-12]

This book is dedicated to my daughter, Giavrielle Sarahannah Lightfoot.
Do know that this book and all that I do, I do for you.

—Johnathan Lightfoot

Contents

14 Searching for Information

What do you think of this book? We want to hear from you!

Microsoft is interested in hearing your feedback so we can continually improve our books and learning resources for you. To participate in a brief online survey, please visit:

www.microsoft.com/learning/booksurvey/

Acknowledgments

First and foremost I want to thank God for the blessings that have been given to me and my family.

Thank you to Microsoft Press and O'Reilly for giving me the opportunity to write this book. Writing a book requires the assistance and experience of a lot of people. Specifically, thanks to my editor Kenyon Brown, technical reviewer Troy Lanphier, copy editor John Pierce, illustrator Robert Romano, vendor coordinator Sumita Mukherji, and production editor Rachel Monaghan for being so patient and helpful throughout the process. Thank you to Mack Sigman with the Federal SharePoint User Group (FEDSPUG); I could not have produced the screenshots or delved so deeply into the SharePoint 2010 platform so quickly without your help. Special thank you to Dux Raymond Sy for your words of encouragement and for making me rethink how things are done within the SharePoint platform.

Thank you to the U.S. Navy for taking a young man over 20 years ago and showing me that anything is possible as long as one is willing to work hard and adhere to the core values of honor, courage, and commitment. Go Navy, Beat Army! Also, thank you to all of my past colleagues and business users at Electronic Data Systems, Norwegian Cruise Line, and Hawaiian Telcom—each of you in your own special way helped me to become the person that I am today.

A really big thank you to my wife, Genevievette—thank you for the encouragement during the long nights and early mornings while working with the SharePoint platform and on this book. Without your sacrifices, commitment, and dedication, there is no way that I would be where I am today.

—Johnathan Lightfoot

1

About This Book

If you want to get the most from your computer and your software with the least amount of time and effort—and who doesn't?—this book is for you. You'll find *Microsoft SharePoint 2010 Plain & Simple* to be a straightforward, easy-to-read reference tool. With the premise that your computer should work for you, not you for it, this book's purpose is to help you get your work done quickly and efficiently so that you can get away from the computer and live your life.

No Computerspeak!

If you are like most people, you have enough things to remember with just accomplishing your job tasks on a day-to-day basis. The last thing you want to do is learn a new occupation in order to get your current tasks completed. In this book we outline over a hundred operations that you could be called upon to do within the SharePoint 2010 platform.

Let's face it—when there's a task you don't know how to do but you need to get it done in a hurry, or when you're stuck in the middle of a task and can't figure out what to do next, there's nothing more frustrating than having to read page after page of technical background material. You want the information you need—nothing more, nothing less—and you want it now! *And* it should be easy to find and understand.

That's what this book is all about. It's written in plain English—not technical jargon. No single task in the book takes more than a few pages. Just look up the task in the index or the table of contents and turn to the page, and there's the information you need, laid out in an illustrated step-by-step format. You don't get bogged down by the whys and wherefores: Just follow the steps and get your work done.

Occasionally you might have to turn to another page if the procedure you're working on is accompanied by a *See Also* that refers you to a related task. Tasks might also contain some useful *Tips* here and there, point out some features that are new in SharePoint 2010, or include a *Try This* or a *Caution* that warns you of a potential problem.

But in the end we have written this book avoiding the use of technical terms. It is our sincere hope that this book will be your first resource to go to when you need to get a task done.

Just Essential Tasks

The SharePoint platform is large and can be customized and morphed into numerous configurations. The purpose of this book is to show you some of the more common tasks that you will come across.

The sections and tasks in this book are organized logically for the types of things you use SharePoint 2010 to accomplish. If you have never used SharePoint, you can start at the beginning of the book and work through the chapters in order to become comfortable with all the essential features of SharePoint. However, if you know exactly what you want to accomplish, just find the tasks and follow the steps.

...And the Easiest Way to Do Them

SharePoint 2010 uses the same ribbon interface introduced in Microsoft Office 2007 and extended in Microsoft Office 2010. Although there are often multiple ways to complete the same task in SharePoint, we have given preference to using commands and options provided on the ribbon to take advantage of the familiarity most users have with the ribbon and reinforce the consistency this brings to Microsoft applications. That said, however, there will be times when we show you faster ways that do not require the ribbon. Just know that we are trying to show you the easiest way to accomplish your task.

A Quick Overview

SharePoint is most commonly used in business environments, and its installation and support require technical expertise that is beyond the scope of this book to describe. Your first exposure to SharePoint will probably be in your workplace where SharePoint has been set up and initially configured or supported by your company's IT department, or possibly through a hosted implementation such as Microsoft Share-Point Online. In this light, this book does not start with the details of installing or configuring the SharePoint platform. Instead, the materials focus on getting you up to speed using the features that SharePoint provides to help manage information and collaborate with colleagues.

Section 2 covers what's new in SharePoint 2010. This section informs those of you with a pretty good understanding of previous versions of SharePoint about the new and exciting capabilities that are in SharePoint 2010, as well as improvements.

Section 3 introduces SharePoint sites and quickly gets you started using the capabilities of SharePoint 2010. In this section you learn how to create and configure a basic SharePoint site and how to customize site themes and navigation menus. You also learn how to save your customizations as a template that can be used to create additional sites.

Section 4 covers some of the more advanced features that can help you better manage information in SharePoint sites within your organization. In this section you learn how you can configure content types and site columns to capture information stored in SharePoint lists and libraries. You learn how you can customize document creation with templates and enhance collaboration and content management with work-flow capabilities.

Sections 5 and 6 cover the fundamentals of how you most commonly use SharePoint 2010 for working with content. SharePoint lists and libraries are used to store and collaborate on documents and other types of information, like calendars and tasks. In Section 5 you learn how to use the ribbon menu of lists and libraries to access the content management features of SharePoint and how to customize the display of information with views. Section 6 provides additional details related to working with documents and records.

Section 7 covers the specialized features SharePoint offers for working with media assets such as video, audio, and images, including how to upload and stream video and audio and configure image slide shows.

Section 8 goes over the powerful information management policies that come with SharePoint 2010—features such as auditing, document labels, document bar codes, and expiration policies. By using these features you can get a hold of your content and manage it a lot more effectively than in the past.

Section 9 focuses on the how SharePoint can help organize people and processes with support for project tasks, issues, and group discussion lists. You learn how SharePoint provides special integration with Microsoft Project, a desktop project management application.

Section 10 explains how to gain an even greater level of functionality and ease of use by extending and integrating SharePoint 2010 with Microsoft Office on desktop computers and mobile devices. You also learn about a special feature that allows broadcasting PowerPoint presentations.

Section 11 helps you create and publish content using SharePoint blog sites. Blogs are a popular approach to capturing and publishing information by using short and informal posts that can be organized using categories and allow reader feedback to be captured as ratings and comments.

Section 12 covers one of the most important aspects of SharePoint—security. In this section we go over security levels, creating groups, inheritance, and inviting people to your SharePoint site.

Section 13 expands on the capabilities of SharePoint blogs covered in Section 11, with guidance on how to use the advanced social networking features found in the SharePoint Standard and Enterprise Server editions. You learn how to configure a personal profile that can include a picture, contact information, professional expertise, and other information.

You also learn how to track and share information with colleagues using a personal note board and content tags.

Finally, in Section 14, we offer information on the powerful search capabilities of SharePoint that help you find information stored in sites created across your organization, including advanced search features available only in the SharePoint Standard and Enterprise Server editions or a very advanced search edition called Microsoft FAST Search Server 2010 for SharePoint. SharePoint search features include the ability to use special keywords, wildcards, and property filters; refine your search results using attributes like author, last modified date, and other metadata; and subscribe to search results as an RSS feed that can keep you up to date on content being added to SharePoint that matches previous searches.

A Few Assumptions

To write a book, you have to first think about your readers. Who are they, what do they already know, and what do they need to know? SharePoint is first and foremost a Web application designed for business users to collaborate and manage documents and other information. You may have been asked to use SharePoint while working on a company project or for sharing documents with colleagues in your department at work. Or maybe you are a small business owner who is looking to use a hosted version of SharePoint to help your employees store and share information.

In writing this book, we assumed that you are using a laptop or desktop computer with access to a business network or remote access to a SharePoint site over the Internet. We assume you are computer literate and have a basic knowledge of how to use your local computer, such as turning it on and starting programs, and are comfortable using the standard menus and commands of a Web browser to open, view, and interact with Web applications.

In addition, SharePoint is part of an integrated suite of technologies from Microsoft referred to as the Office System, which includes the Microsoft Office desktop productivity tools (such as Word, Excel, PowerPoint, and Outlook, depending on the edition). Although having Microsoft Office installed—and having some knowledge of how to use it—is not necessary to benefit from this book, a number of tasks and the entirety of Section 10 make reference to using the integrated features of Microsoft SharePoint and Microsoft Office.

A Final Word (or Two)

This book is designed to make your learning painless, with easy-to-follow steps and plenty of visual information to help you pick things up at a glance. Our goals are to give you what you need, make it easy to find and understand, and help you have fun learning to work with SharePoint 2010. The best way to learn is by *doing*, and that's how we hope you'll use this book.

We would also encourage you to attend training sessions whenever possible in order to enhance your understanding of the SharePoint 2010 platform. While we have endeavored to provide you with the information that you need to accomplish some of the more common tasks that you could be called upon to do, we also believe that with additional training you can come up with even more creative solutions to challenges you may be faced with in your organization.

What's New and Improved in SharePoint 2010?

When Microsoft introduced SharePoint 2010 at the SharePoint Conference in October 2009, developers, administrators and IT professionals must have felt that Christmas had come early. The SharePoint 2010 platform was greatly enhanced over previous versions of the platform. A lot of the enhancements were inspired by the comments and suggestions of the very people who use it every day.

This section is where you will get your first look at SharePoint 2010 and will be able to see some of the changes that have been implemented. Because the number of changes and upgrades are just too plentiful to go into completely within the scope of this book, we will focus on the features that affect the end-user experience.

We will describe the changes and what they will mean to you in terms of getting your work done more efficiently. In later chapters we will delve more deeply into some of the enhancements, showing you how to best utilize these changes in order to make your life easier.

New Functionality

Some of the features introduced in Microsoft SharePoint 2010 were put in place because of customer requests, and quite a few are simply an evolution of the SharePoint platform. In the end, the functionality was added to provide a richer experience to the user base.

Microsoft Access Services

You can now create, edit, and update Microsoft Access 2010 databases within SharePoint. These databases can be viewed and manipulated by using a Web browser, the Microsoft Access client, or a Web page that is linked to your site.

Business Connectivity Services

It is now possible to easily connect to external data sources. By using Office 2010, you are able to update external data sources to create, read, update, and delete (CRUD) items.

Digital Asset Manager

SharePoint 2010 has a library dedicated to managing and sharing digital assets such as audio, video, and other rich media files.

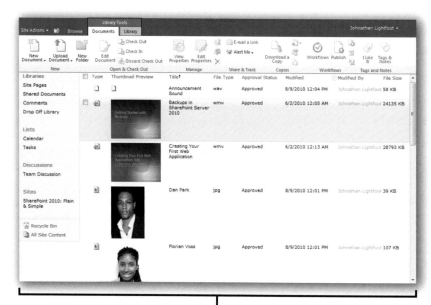

With the Digital Assets library, multiple rich media files can be stored together

Read-Only Databases

SharePoint 2010 now has the ability to set up read-only databases. This is important for upgrades or server maintenance. During these evolutions users are still able to access and view their content. By having this feature there will be less downtime for you during IT operations.

Records Management

Separate locations in which to store records in SharePoint 2010 do not have to be created. Records can be managed in an archive or in the same library or list (in place). When content is declared a record, different policies can be applied to it than are applied to active content (for example, make the content read-only), while maintaining the content in an active list or library.

Microsoft Visio Services

SharePoint 2010 gives you the ability to share and view Microsoft Visio diagrams within a Web browser. It also enables data-connected Visio 2010 diagrams to be refreshed and updated from a variety of data sources (also using the browser).

Coauthoring

SharePoint now supports simultaneous multiuser collaboration, meaning that multiple people can edit the same document at the same time.

Microsoft recommends a maximum number of 10 coauthors. You can have up to 99 coauthors on the same document, but performance will be degraded.

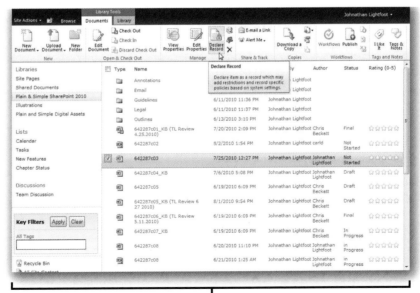

With SharePoint 2010, you can now store declared records in an active library

Windows 7 Search

You can now search SharePoint sites directly using the desktop search functionality of the Windows 7 operating system.

Tag Profiles

Find information and discussions on specific keywords or topics using Tag Profile pages.

Chart Web Parts

You can now create charts within a browser based on data in SharePoint lists. You can also use business connectivity and Excel Services–based lists to support these Web Parts.

Improved Functionality

Besides introducing many new features, SharePoint 2010 also has improved functionality that was present in the previous version of SharePoint.

User Interface

The out-of-the-box interface for SharePoint 2010 uses the ribbon interface found in Microsoft Office clients such as Word and Excel. Including the ribbon in SharePoint 2010 brings continuity to the Office products and also makes it easier and faster to find the functionality you are looking for.

Enterprise Search

It is now possible for administrators to configure a search infrastructure that can help business users find information in the enterprise quickly and efficiently.

Document Ribbon

Contextual tab
Tab

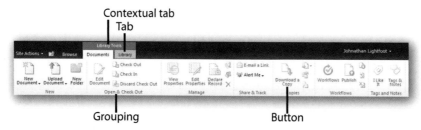

Grouping   Button

Library/ List Ribbon

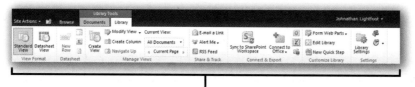

The ribbon user interface makes it easier to find the tools that you need faster

Excel Services

With Microsoft SharePoint Server 2010 you can load, calculate, and display Microsoft Excel workbooks using Excel Services.

By using Excel Services, you can reuse and share Excel workbooks on SharePoint Server 2010 portals and dashboards. For example, accountants, analysts, or engineers can create content in Excel and share it with others by using an SharePoint Server 2010 portal and dashboard—without writing custom code. You can control what data is displayed, and you can maintain a single version of your Excel workbook.

Large List Scalability and Management

SharePoint 2010 supports lists that can contain millions of items. Administrators are able to control the number of items returned so that searches do not slow down SharePoint.

Microsoft does not recommend having more than 30 million items in a list or library.

Improved Backup and Restore

Through the use of Windows PowerShell, SharePoint 2010 can back up or restore not only the farm but also farm configuration information, site collections, subsites, or lists.

Administrators can now respond to user needs more quickly and with greater flexibility.

Themes

Themes provide the ability for users to change the look and feel of their sites. Themes can be used to help sites more closely match an organization's branding requirements.

New Interface for customizing themes

PerformancePoint Services

You now have the ability to create scorecards that bring together data from multiple sources both inside and outside SharePoint 2010. PerformancePoint Services can produce interactive, context-driven dashboards to track the KPIs (key performance indicators) of your organization.

Social Computing

SharePoint 2010 has improved My Site Web sites and social technologies such as blogs, wikis, and RSS (Really Simple Syndication) feeds.

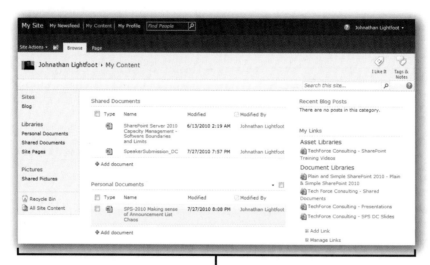

Personal SharePoint site referred to as My Site

Microsoft Word Automation Services

You can now save, export, and print Word documents from SharePoint. This functionality also helps you create, manipulate, and render documents.

SharePoint Workspaces

Microsoft has changed the name of Microsoft Office Groove to Microsoft SharePoint Workspace. With this product, you can take lists, libraries, line-of-business data, and even entire sites offline. Work locally, and SharePoint Workspace 2010 can synchronize your offline changes with the server when you reconnect to the network.

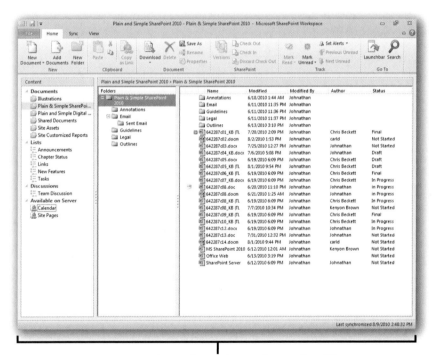

SharePoint site copied into SharePoint Workspace for offline access

Getting Started with SharePoint Sites

Microsoft SharePoint 2010 is a Web-based platform that is used for collaboration among team members working on various projects. Because SharePoint is a Web-based program, a supported browser is really the only piece of software that is needed to access and utilize the many features that SharePoint provides.

A SharePoint site is a Web site that is used for organizing various aspects of your project. For example, you can have a SharePoint site that is used for the composition of proposals. This site might contain various items, such as an announcement list to keep the team informed of any news that could affect a proposal being worked on. It might also have various document libraries that can contain reference documents and guiding principles for proposals, along with other tools that the team needs to put proposals together.

An immediate benefit to using SharePoint sites is the centralization of information. If you use a SharePoint site you have a central location where you can access, work with, and collaborate on different aspects of a project. Gone will be the days of having to search through your e-mail for an important attachment, access file shares to locate different documents, or guess whether the information you have is the most current.

Understanding Sites

Usually, a SharePoint administrator performs the installation, configuration, and deployment of SharePoint throughout your organization. Part of this process is establishing something called the top-level site. It is through the top-level site that subsites (or sites) are created. It is beyond the scope of this book to go into detail about the various scenarios that can be implemented to get SharePoint up and running. However, remember that once the top-level site is created, then subsites can be created.

Each site has a site administrator (or two) assigned to it. The site administrator's duties can include granting access to the site, creating lists and libraries, and creating additional sites, to name a few. One of the great things about SharePoint is that it gives you the ability to assign various responsibilities to various people within your team.

Once a site administrator has the Web address for a site, the administrator can customize the site and apply security settings to it that allow people to access the site.

Access a SharePoint Site

(1) Type the Web address for the SharePoint site you want to access, and then press Enter.

Try This!

If you have a SharePoint site that you can access, type the site's Web address in your browser's address bar.

Creating a SharePoint Site Based on a Template

Site administrators have a lot of latitude for how they can create a site. They can choose to create a blank site and add different components to the site, or they can employ a site template to assist them with creating the site. If you have used a template in Word, Excel, or any other Office program, the concept is the same in SharePoint. A template is a starting point that you can use to quickly produce a site that has the basics of what your team needs. This saves you time, but it also ensures a certain level of consistency for SharePoint sites throughout your organization.

SharePoint 2010 comes with numerous site templates that are ready to be used out of the box.

Template Name	Description
Assets Web Database	An assets database to keep track of assets, including asset details and owners.
Basic Meeting Workspace	A site that you can use to plan, organize, and capture the results of a meeting. It provides lists for managing the meeting's agenda, meeting attendees, and documents.
Basic Search Center	A site that provides search functionality. The site includes pages for search results and advanced searches.
Blank Meeting Workspace	A blank meeting site that you can customize according to your own requirements.
Blank Site	A blank site that you can customize to meet your requirements.
Blog	A site that a person or team can use to post ideas, observations, and expertise that site visitors can comment on.
Business Intelligence Center	A site for presenting business intelligence data. It provides document libraries for storing documents, images, data connections, and dashboard Web Parts. It also provides lists for linking content from PerformancePoint Services in Microsoft SharePoint Server 2010.

Template Name	Description
Charitable Contributions Web Database	A database to track information about fundraising campaigns, including donations, campaign-related events, and pending tasks.
Contacts Web Database	A contacts database to manage information about people that your team works with, such as customers and partners.
Decision Meeting Workspace	A site you can use to track the status of issues or make decisions at meetings. It provides lists to create tasks, store documents, and record decisions.
Document Center	A site that can be used to centrally manage documents in your organization.
Document Workspace	A site on which colleagues can work together on a document. It provides a document library for storing the primary document and supporting files, a tasks list for assigning to-do items, and a links list to point to resources that are related to the document.

Template Name	Description
Enterprise Search Center	A site that provides search functionality. The Welcome page includes a search box that has two tabs, one for general searches and another for searches for information about people. You can add and customize tabs to focus on other search scopes or result types.
Enterprise Wiki	A site that can be used to publish knowledge that you capture and want to share across an enterprise. It provides an easy content-editing experience in a single location for coauthoring content, for discussions, and for managing projects.
Group Work Site	This template provides a groupware solution that teams can use to create, organize, and share information. It includes a group calendar, a circulation list, a phone call memo list, a document library, and the other basic lists.
Issues Web Database	An issues database to manage a set of issues or problems. You can assign, prioritize, and follow the progress of issues from start to finish.
Microsoft Project Site	A site that supports team collaboration on projects. This site includes project documents, project issues, project risks, and project deliverables lists that can be linked to tasks in Microsoft Project Server 2010.
Multipage Meeting Workspace	A site on which you can plan a meeting and capture the meeting's decisions and other results. It provides lists for managing the agenda and meeting attendees. It also provides two blank pages that you can customize based on your requirements.

Template Name	Description
My Site Host	A site that hosts personal sites (My Sites) and the public People Profile page. This template has to be provisioned only once per user profile service application. This template is available only at the site collection level.
Personalization Site	A site for delivering personalized views, data, and navigation from a site collection to My Site. It includes Web Parts that are specific to personalization and navigation that are optimized for My Site sites. This template is available only at the site level.
PowerPoint Broadcast Center	A site for hosting Microsoft PowerPoint 2010 broadcasts. Presenters can connect to the site and create a link for remote viewers to watch a slide show in a Web browser.
Projects Web Database	A project tracking database to track multiple projects and assign tasks to different people.
Publishing Portal	A starter site hierarchy that you can use for an Internet site or a large intranet portal. You can use distinctive branding to customize this site. It includes a home page, a sample press releases site, a Search Center, and a logon page. Typically, this site has many more readers than contributors, and it is used for publishing Web pages by following approval workflows. This site enables content approval workflows, by default, for a more formal and controlled publishing process. It also restricts the rights of anonymous users so that they can see content pages but not see SharePoint Server 2010 application pages. This template is available only at the site collection level.

Template Name	Description
Publishing Site	A blank site for expanding your Web site and quickly publishing Web pages. Contributors can work on draft versions of pages and publish them to make them visible to readers. This site includes document and image libraries for storing Web publishing assets.
Publishing Site with Workflow	A site for publishing Web pages on a schedule by using approval workflows. It includes document and image libraries for storing Web publishing assets. By default, only sites based on this template can be created under this site. This template is available only at the site level when the Publishing Portal template is used to create the top-level site.
Records Center	A site that is designed for records management. Records managers can configure the routing table to direct incoming files to specific locations. The site also enables you to manage whether records can be deleted or modified after they are added to the repository.
Social Meeting Workspace	A site on which you can plan social occasions. It provides lists for tracking attendees, providing directions, and storing pictures of the event.
Team Site	A site on which a team can organize, author, and share information. It provides a document library and lists for managing announcements, calendar items, tasks, and discussions.

Template Name	Description
Visio Process Repository	A site on which teams can view, share, and store Microsoft Visio process diagrams. It provides a versioned document library for storing process diagrams and lists for managing announcements, tasks, and review discussions.

As you can see, SharePoint 2010 comes with a number of built-in templates to help you get your SharePoint site running as quickly as possible. Among the different templates, the Team Site template contains a very good sampling of lists and libraries that are available for team-collaboration scenarios. Because of this, the Team Site template is the most commonly used template within organizations.

Creating a team site in SharePoint 2010 is even easier than in previous releases. When you select the New Site option from the Site Actions menu, you are presented with the templates that you can choose as the basis for your site. After you select a template, you simply have to enter a title for the site along with the URL for the site.

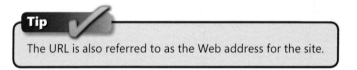

Tip

The URL is also referred to as the Web address for the site.

Create a Site Based on the Team Site Template

(1) Click New Site on the Site Actions menu.

(2) Under All Categories, click Team Site.

(3) Enter a title for the site.

(4) Enter a URL for the site.

(5) Click Create.

Try This!

We use a team site for most of the examples in this book. Create a team site that you can use to follow along with the examples in the book.

Tip ✓

When entering the URL you only need to specify what the site name (last portion of the URL) will be. SharePoint will automatically generate the first portion of the URL.

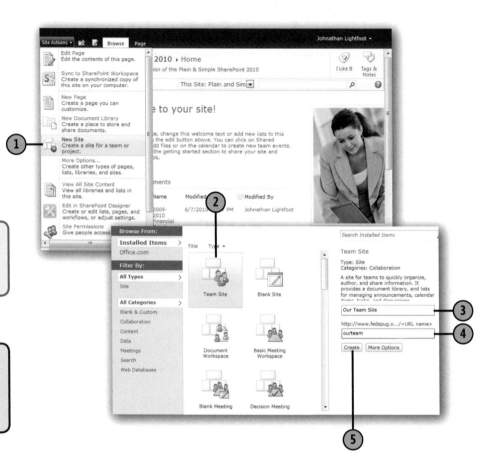

Locating Items on a Team Site

As mentioned in the previous section, the Team Site template offers a good sampling of the capabilities in SharePoint. As such, this template is one that you will most likely see deployed in several locations of your organization.

A team site comes with announcements lists, discussion boards, document libraries, a calendar, a links list, a wiki page library, and a task list already configured and ready for use. These components of the site allow you and your team to quickly set up and begin collaborating on your projects.

After you have a team site set up, it's good to go over where everything is located.

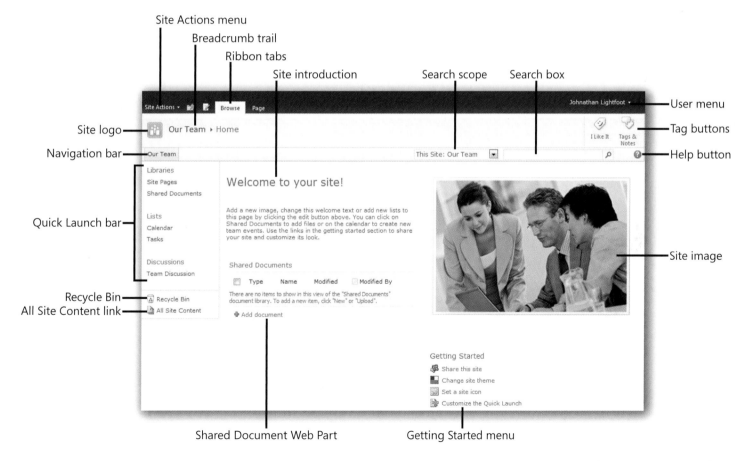

Site Actions menu
Breadcrumb trail
Ribbon tabs
Site introduction
Search scope
Search box
User menu
Site logo
Tag buttons
Navigation bar
Help button
Quick Launch bar
Site image
Recycle Bin
All Site Content link
Shared Document Web Part
Getting Started menu

Working with Workspaces

In addition to sites, you can also work with workspaces in SharePoint. Where a site may be used by your department as the central location for keeping up with projects that your department as a whole is working on, a workspace is usually dedicated to one specific item or task.

In SharePoint 2010, you can use two different types of workspaces: a Meeting Workspace and a Document Workspace. Meeting Workspaces are for single meetings. Inside these workspaces you can keep track of assigned tasks, attendance, the agenda, and other meeting-related content. A Document Workspace is set up for the compilation of a single document. You can have secondary documents related to the document you are preparing, along with reference materials and discussion boards your team can use to help create the document.

Create a Document Workspace

1. Click New Site on the Site Actions menu.

2. Click Document Workspace.

3. Type a title for the workspace.

4. Type the last portion of the Web address you want to use.

5. Click Create.

Changing a Site's Look and Feel

Chances are good that when you start to use your SharePoint site, you will want to customize a few things to meet the needs of your team. SharePoint 2010 has expanded capabilities over the previous release that allow you to do many of the customizations within the browser.

Some things you might want to change include the title, description, and icon for the site. You might also want to specify whether the Quick Launch bar is shown or whether to display a tree view of your site instead. You might also want to change the color scheme of your site. Through the browser interface in SharePoint, you can make these changes very easily.

Change the Title and Description of Your Site

① Click Site Settings on the Site Action menu.

② Click Title, Description, And Icon in the Look And Feel group.

③ Change the title.

④ Change the description.

⑤ Click OK.

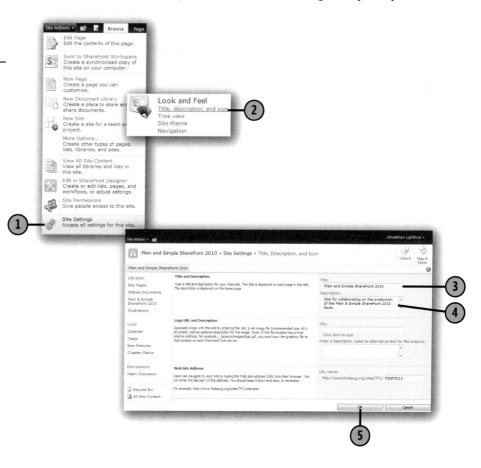

> **Tip** ✓
>
> Through this procedure you can also change the site icon. Be advised that you need to upload the picture you want to use to a library to obtain a Web address for it. For more information, see "Upload Files to an Asset Library" on page 103.

> **Tip** ✓
>
> In addition to using the built-in capabilities of SharePoint, you can use Microsoft SharePoint Designer 2010 and Microsoft Visual Studio 2010 to customize your site in greater detail.

Turn Off the Quick Launch Bar

(1) Click Site Settings on the Site Actions menu.

(2) Click Tree View in the Look And Feel group.

(3) Clear the Enable Quick Launch check box.

(4) Click OK.

Try This!

You may find that your team does not like the Quick Launch bar and would prefer to use the Windows tree view instead. Try enabling the tree view option for your site.

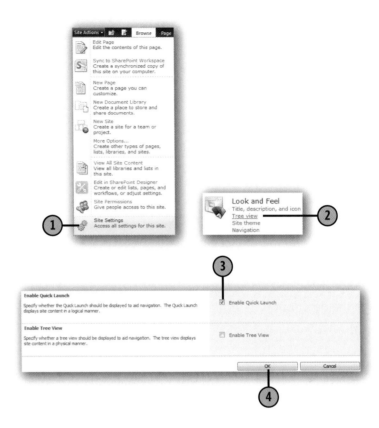

Change the Color Theme of the Site

1. Click Site Settings on the Site Actions menu.

2. Click Site Theme in the Look And Feel group.

3. Select the theme that you want to use.

4. Click Apply.

Try This!

SharePoint 2010 comes with several preconfigured themes for you to choose from. You can also personalize different page elements individually. Instead of using a preconfigured theme, try selecting the color and fonts for your site on your own.

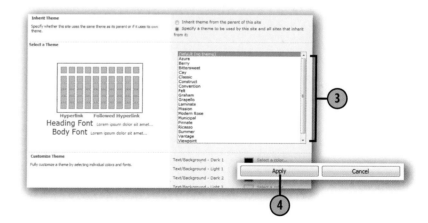

Viewing Site Content

One of the most common navigation options used in Share-Point is the Quick Launch bar. By default, whenever a new library, list, survey, or other object is created in SharePoint, it is listed on the Quick Launch bar. However, if you have a rather large site, the administrator might decide not to list every object on the Quick Launch bar. If you have 30 items on the Quick Launch bar, you can imagine how difficult finding objects becomes.

If you cannot locate what you are looking for on the Quick Launch bar, you can always use the All Site Content option located below the Quick Launch bar. By using this option you can see all the different items that are available on your site.

View All Site Content

① Click All Site Content.

② View the different objects available to you.

Tip

What you see on the All Site Content option depends on your security level. If you have access to an item, you see it listed; if you don't have access, the item isn't listed.

Saving a Site Template

After you create a site and set it up the way you need it to be, you might decide to copy it to use as a template for sites that you create in the future. By saving your newly created site as a template you can make deploying sites like it much easier because you don't need to re-create them manually.

When you save a site as a template, any lists, libraries, or other objects you have added are also saved. You also have the option of saving some content with the template. For example, maybe in each of your newly created sites you want to have certain forms uploaded to specific libraries during the site creation process.

Save a Site as a Template

(1) Click Site Settings on the Site Actions menu.

(2) Click Save Site As Template in the Site Actions Group.

(3) Type a file name for the template.

(4) Type a template name to identify the template for when someone creates a new site.

(5) Type a description.

(6) Select the Include Content check box if you want to include the content on the site in the template.

(7) Click OK.

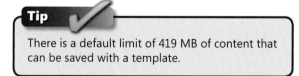

Tip

There is a default limit of 419 MB of content that can be saved with a template.

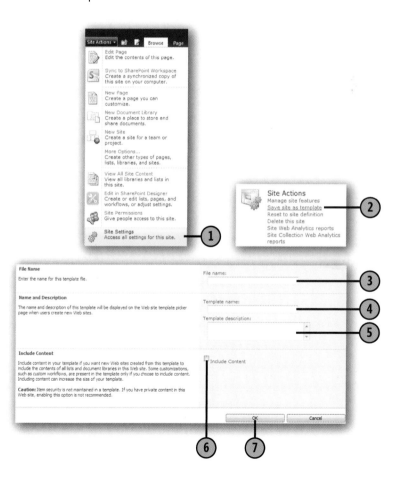

4

Organizing and Managing Information

With all the content that you can have in your Microsoft SharePoint 2010 site, it is important that you be able to organize and manage it. What sets SharePoint apart from file-sharing programs are its features for managing and organizing content. After all, with a file-sharing program, you are limited to creating folders and storing documents in the folders. What you can't do is set up policies for what to do with the content after a certain amount of time or easily find relevant documents that you need for a project, especially if they are spread throughout several different folders.

In this section, we explain the out-of-the-box features that you can use to organize and manage content. We also show you some of the improved features introduced with SharePoint 2010, including content types and site columns.

Introducing Site Columns and Content Types

As you produce content, you will want to locate and manage that information in the fastest and easiest ways possible. By using metadata, you can store vital pieces of information concerning your content. This metadata is then available to you to manage and organize your content. In SharePoint, metadata is referred to as *site columns*.

A site column is a column definition or template that can be used in multiple lists and libraries across multiple SharePoint sites. Site columns are useful because they reduce the amount of work you need to do when you create lists and libraries. Site columns also help ensure the consistency of the metadata collected across sites. For example, you can define a site column named Artist. Users can then add the column to their lists and libraries, and this ensures that the attributes you set up for this column are the same (at least in the beginning) in each list or library that it appears in.

Content types are a group of settings that describe the shared behaviors for a specific type of content. Content types can also be used across sites. For example, during the course of a project your team might produce different kinds of content, such as receipts, legal documents, purchase orders, and memos. Although you might store these items together because they are all related to the project, they are each created, utilized, shared, and retained differently. You can define a content type for each item type to ensure the consistency of the metadata that is captured and to ensure that each piece is handled according to your organization's business processes.

A content type can contain the following:

- Columns that you want to assign to items of a certain type
- A document template on which you want to base any new items of a certain type
- Custom New, Edit, or Display forms that can be used for the creation of content.
- Workflows
- Custom features

Content types give your team the ability to manage and organize content consistently across lists and libraries within a site collection. Site columns and content types are related because content types can contain site columns. By adding a site column to a content type, you can quickly set up the content type consistently within your site.

SharePoint 2010 comes with several out-of-the-box content types.

Content Type	Description
Business Intelligence	
Excel-Based Status Indicator	Create a status indicator using data from Excel Services
Fixed-Value-Based Status Indicator	Create a status indicator using manually entered information
Report	Create a report using basic report information
SharePoint List–Based Status Indicator	Create a status indicator using data from SharePoint lists
SQL Server Analysis Services–Based Status Indicator	Create a status indicator using data from SQL Server Analysis Services
Web Part Page with Status List	Create a page that displays status indicators and Excel workbooks
Content Organizer Content Type	
Rule	Create a rule that moves content submitted to a site to the correct library or folder

Content Type	Description
Digital Asset Content Types	
Audio	Upload an audio file
Image	Upload an image file
Rich Media Asset	Upload an asset (for Java or Silverlight applications)
Video	Upload a video
Document Content Types	
Basic Page	Create a basic page
Document	Create a document
Dublin Core Columns	The Dublin Core metadata element set
Form	Create a basic form
Link to a Document	Create a link to a document in a different location
List View Style	Create a list view style
Master Page	Create a master page
Picture	Upload an image or photograph
Web Part Page	Create a Web Part Page
Wiki Page	Create a Wiki page

Content Type	Description
List Content Types	
Announcement	Create a new news item, status, or other short piece of information
Comment	Create a new blog comment
Contact	Store information about a business or personal contact
East Asia Contact	Store information about a business or personal contact (uses East Asian formatting)
Event	Create a new meeting, deadline, or other event
Issue	Track an issue or problem
Item	Create a list item
Link	Create a link to a Web page or other resource
Message	Create a message
Post	Create a blog post
Reservations	Reserve a resource
Schedule	Create an appointment
Schedule and Reservations	Create an appointment and reserve a resource
Task	Track a work item that you or your team needs to complete

Content Type	Description
Folder Content Types	
Discussion	Create a discussion topic
Folder	Create a folder
Summary Task	Group and describe related tasks that you or your team needs to complete
Group Work Content Types	
Circulation	Add a new circulation
Holiday	Add a new holiday
New Word	Add a new word to a list
Official Notice	Add a new official notice
Phone Call Memo	Add a new phone call memo
Resource	Add a new resource
Resource Group	Add a new resource group
Timecard	Add new timecard data
Users	Add new users to a list
What's New Notification	Add a new What's New notification
Special Content Types	
Unknown Document Types	Allows users to upload documents of any content type to a library; unknown document types are treated as their original content type in client applications

Managing Site Columns

You can use site columns in various sites, lists, libraries, or individual items; thereby ensuring that you capture the information you need consistently across your site. For example, suppose you are required to collect status information for certain documents. By creating a Status site column, you can apply the column to other lists that capture information concerning documents. In the end, you will have collected status information about documents no matter where they are on your site.

SharePoint 2010 comes with several predefined site columns. You can also create your own. You should become familiar with the built-in columns so that you know what type of metadata is available with each of them.

You might need to create your own site columns to capture metadata unique to your organization. SharePoint 2010 provides a very easy interface for doing this. After you define a site column, it is available on your site and on any child sites that are created in the future.

You might also have situations arise in which you don't need to create a completely new site column. For example, perhaps a site column exists that generally fits your needs, but you need it altered a bit to fit exactly. SharePoint 2010 gives you this ability, but you have to remember that any changes you make to a site column affect current and future deployments of the site column.

In this section, we show you how to open, browse, create, and edit site columns.

Open Site Columns

① Click Site Settings on the Site Actions menu.

② Click Site Columns in the Galleries section.

Tip

Site columns are inherited by child sites from parent sites, so most of the columns that you see originate from the site collection that is the parent site.

Site columns are divided into several groups

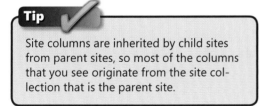

Browse Site Columns

① Click Site Settings on the Site Actions menu.

② Click Site Columns in the Galleries section.

③ Click the link located in the Source column for the site column you want to browse (if necessary).

④ Click the site column you want to view in the Site Column column.

⑤ After you finish viewing the site column's information, click Cancel.

Tip

Because site columns are inherited from the parent site, you need access to the parent site to browse the information a site column contains. If the site column you want to browse is located on a parent site, you have to follow the link provided under the Source column to access the site column.

Tip

Remember that site columns are inherited from the parent site. It is not unusual to see that the source for most of your site columns originates from your top-level site.

Try This!

Browse the site column information for the Anniversary site column.

Tip

It is a good idea to have a look at the information that the predefined site columns contain because several have similar names but capture different types of information.

Create a Site Column

① Open the Site Columns page (see "Browse Site Columns" on page 32).

② Click Create.

③ Enter a name for the new column.

④ Select the type of information the column will contain.

⑤ Select the group that you want the column to be categorized with.

⑥ Enter any additional information that you need to.

⑦ Click OK.

Tip

The settings in the Additional Column Settings section depend on the type of data you choose for the column in the Name And Type section.

Try This!

After you return to the Site Columns page, go to the Show Group section and select the group name that you associated your column with. Notice that your column is listed.

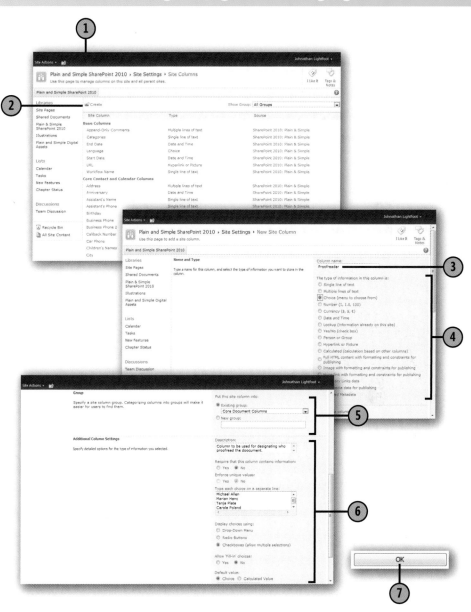

Edit Site Columns

① Open the Site Columns page (see "Browse Site Columns" on page 32).

② From the Show Group list, select the group that the column is associated with, and click the site column.

③ Make your changes to the column.

④ Click OK.

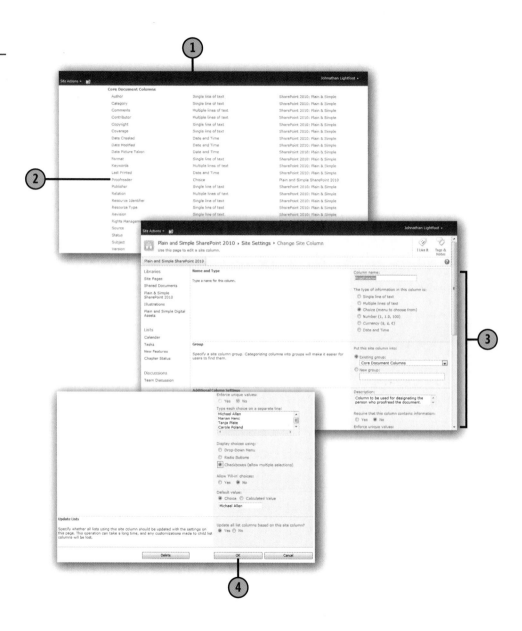

Managing Content Types

In addition to site columns, SharePoint 2010 provides content types for managing and organizing content. Content types are a group of settings that describe the shared behaviors for a specific type of content. Like site columns, content types are reusable, and they are commonly used to capture data elements for items uploaded or created within a document library.

Once created, content types can be accessed not only in the site in which they were created but also in child sites and across an entire site collection. In this section, we show you how to access and inspect content types.

Access Content Types

① Click Site Settings on the Site Actions menu.

② Click Site Content Types in the Galleries section.

Inspect Content Types

1 Click Site Settings on the Site Actions menu.

2 Click Site Content Types.

3 Click the link for the content type.

4 Scroll through the different attributes of the content type.

Try This!

Inspect the Phone Call Memo content type.

Customizing Document Templates with Content Types

Organizations need the ability to manage their content. Toward this end, organizations have used document templates extensively. By using document templates, organizations can ensure consistency within their various forms of content.

The issues today, however, are finding content when it's needed and being able to properly collect, organize, manage, and control the content. By associating document templates with content types, organizations can better perform these tasks.

In this section we show you how to associate a document template with a content type.

Associate a Document Template with a Content Type

① Click Site Settings on the Site Actions menu.

② Click Site Content Types.

③ Click the site content type you want to associate with a template.

④ Click Advanced Settings.

⑤ Select the document template you want to use.

- You can enter the URL of an existing document template if you have it stored in a document library in SharePoint.

- You can upload the template from your computer or another location.

⑥ Click OK.

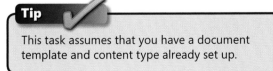

Tip ✓

This task assumes that you have a document template and content type already set up.

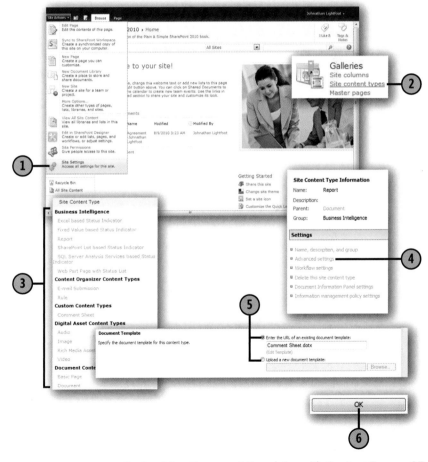

Working with Workflows

In today's world of oversight, regulation, and compliance, organizations have had to implement business processes to comply with ever-growing requirements. At the same time, people are being asked to collaborate more effectively and efficiently. Workflows enable you to automate tasks; thus ensuring that business processes are handled in a consistent manner. They also can improve the efficiency and productivity of an organization by managing the tasks and steps that are vital for successful business practice execution.

By associating workflows with a list or library, you enable SharePoint to take over the task of routing documents and items through your organization. When you associate a workflow with an item, the workflow needs a name, a place to post task assignments, and a place to store its history log of events. It also needs to know what conditions need to be met for the workflow to start.

In this section we go over what workflows are; how to associate a workflow with a library, and how to customize workflows for new and modified content.

What Are Workflows?

Workflows have been described several ways; the most common being a series of tasks that end with an outcome you want. When it comes to SharePoint 2010, this a very broad definition of workflows. On the SharePoint 2010 platform, workflows are a lot more specific. Workflows are an automated means of moving documents or items through a predefined series of actions and/or tasks aligned with a business process.

In places we have worked, if you needed a new server set up there was a process you had to follow. This included filling out the proper paperwork for the request, obtaining the proper approving signatures, and then submitting the request to IT for them to perform their work before you finally received your server. This was a manual process in which someone had to "walk" the request through its various stages.

Along the way, delays and disruptions could stop or place the request on hold. With workflows, however, you are able to automate these steps and streamline the process so that the request can be granted faster than before.

SharePoint 2010 comes with several out-of-the-box workflows that are ready for you to use on the first day of your SharePoint deployment. A new feature in SharePoint 2010 is that you can now edit these built-in workflows, which you couldn't do with Microsoft Office SharePoint Server 2007. You are also able to use development tools such as SharePoint Designer 2010, Visual Studio 2010, and even Visio 2010 to create your own custom workflows. What's more, you can associate a workflow with a list, library, content type, or even an entire site!

Associate a Workflow with a Library

1 Click the library with which you want to associate a workflow.

2 Click Library on the Library Tools tab.

3 Click Library Settings.

4 Click Workflow Settings.

(continued on next page)

Tip

Depending on which workflow you select, you might see an additional configuration screen. This screen asks for additional information concerning the workflow, such as who to send e-mail messages to and how to display status messages.

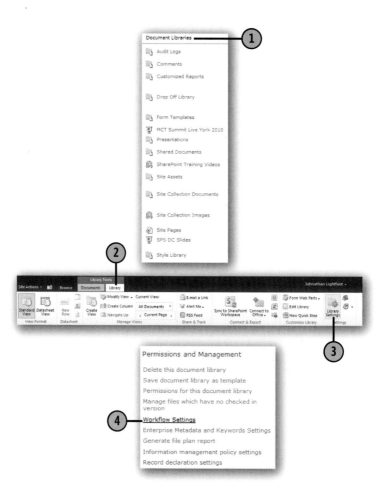

Associate a Workflow with a Library *(continued)*

⑤ Select a workflow template.

⑥ Enter a unique name for the workflow.

⑦ Select a task list in which the workflow should place assigned tasks.

⑧ Select a list for storing the workflow's logs.

⑨ Select options for when the workflow should start.

⑩ Click OK.

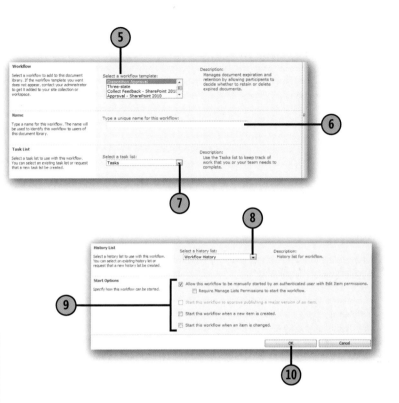

Try This!

Associate the Approval Workflow with either a document library or a list. Specify that the workflow should start when a new item is added, and designate yourself as the person to receive e-mail messages. Now create a new item and observe the workflow as it is processed.

Start a Workflow

① To start a workflow automatically, simply upload a document into a document library that has a workflow associated with it. (See "Uploading Multiple Documents" on page 76.)

② To start a workflow manually, hover over the item for which you want to start the workflow, and click the down arrow.

③ Click Workflows.

④ Click the name of the workflow that you want to start.

⑤ Click Start. (You might have to scroll down to see the Start button.)

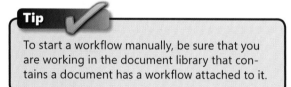

Tip

To start a workflow manually, be sure that you are working in the document library that contains a document has a workflow attached to it.

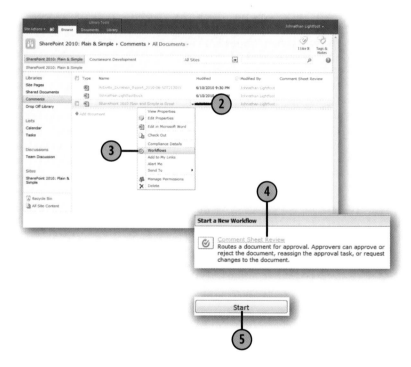

Check the Status of a Running Workflow

1. Verify that a workflow is running (or that its status is In Progress).

2. Click the down arrow for the document you want to check. (You have to hover over the document name to see the down arrow.)

3. Click Workflows.

4. Click the name of the running workflow you want to check.

Try This!

Check to see whether any workflows are running in any of your lists or libraries. If so, check the status of them.

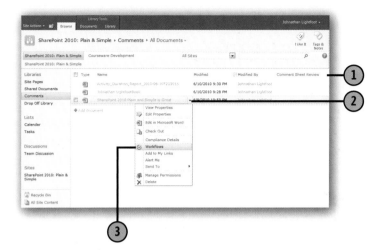

5

List and Library Essentials

Traditionally, organizations have used file servers for storing and retrieving documents, but that's about all organizations can do with file servers. They cannot track changes or views, easily automate document handling processes, or conduct any real management of their documents. Microsoft SharePoint has shown organizations a better way. Through the use of lists and libraries, SharePoint offers true document-management capabilities.

Most people's first experience with SharePoint is through a list or a library. A list is a collection of like items, such as contact information, calendar events, or inventory items. Through the use of lists you can group items for later retrieval. You can also provide a central place where team members have access to the most up-to-date information. Do you remember the last time you needed to poll your team to find the latest contact information for a sales rep, or you had a question about where a meeting was moved to? In SharePoint, you have a central location for this type of information that is current, accurate, and relevant. SharePoint 2010 comes with several lists for collecting different kinds of information, such as tasks, announcements, contacts, and links, to name just a few.

Creating and Deleting Lists

Although SharePoint's site templates provide you with several lists and libraries when you create a site that's based on a template, you more than likely will require additional lists to categorize your information effectively. Maybe you need a list for tracking project tasks or you need a contact list. SharePoint 2010 makes creating and using these lists easy.

On the other hand, a site might have lists that your team does not require. In order to customize the site to meet your team's requirements, you might want to delete any lists that you don't need.

Create a List or Library

(1) Click More Options on the Site Actions menu.

(2) On the Filter By menu, do the following to filter the available template choices:

- Click List or Library to filter the available templates

- Click any category to filter available templates. Click All Categories to view all templates.

(3) Select a list or library template from the list.

(4) Enter a name for your list or library.

(5) Click Create.

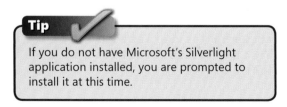

Tip

If you do not have Microsoft's Silverlight application installed, you are prompted to install it at this time.

Delete a List or Library

① Click List or Library on the List Tools or Library Tools tab.

② Click List Settings or Library Settings.

③ Click Delete This List (or Delete This Library).

④ Click OK to confirm you want to send the list to the Recycle Bin.

Try This!

Create a Document Library titled New Library. Once you have it completed, delete it.

Adding, Editing, and Deleting List Items

Individual rows of content in a SharePoint list are called *list items*. SharePoint 2010 can support up to 30 million items in one SharePoint list. Depending on your permission level, you may be able to create, edit, and delete items.

SharePoint also provides you with the ability to attach items to other items. An example is attaching a meeting agenda to a calendar item or a resumé to a job applicants contact list. By default, list items in SharePoint support having one or more attachments; however, attachment support can also be turned off in List Settings for lists where attachment support needs to be restricted.

Add a List Item

① Click All Site Content on the Quick Launch bar.

② Select the list that you want to add items to.

(continued on next page)

Tip

SharePoint can support up to 30 million list items. However, depending on the number of columns you have defined in the list, your results and performance may vary.

Try This!

Add your birthday to the Calendar list.

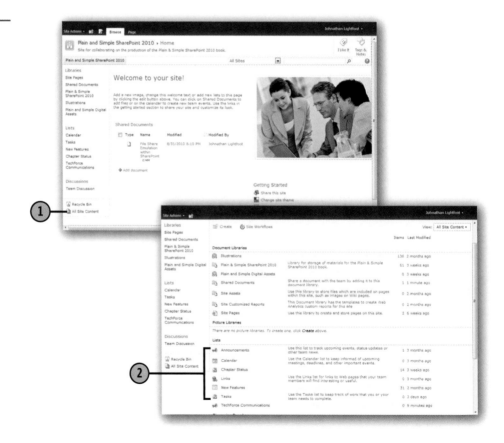

Add a List Item   *(continued)*

③ Click Items on the List Tools tab.

④ Click New Item on the List Tools Items tab.

⑤ Click with the mouse or use the Tab key to move through the item fields and enter data.

⑥ Click Save.

Tip

If you wanted to attach a file to your item you can use the Attach File button on the ribbon to do so.

Tip

A red asterisk designates a required field. You must enter information in this field before SharePoint will save your item.

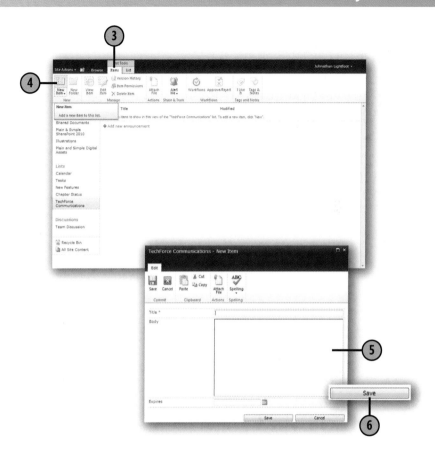

Edit an Item

1. Click Items on the List Tools tab.

2. Click the check box to select an item. (You have to hover over the item to see the check box.)

3. Click Edit Item on the drop-down menu.

4. Click the mouse or use the Tab key to navigate between fields and edit properties.

5. Click Save.

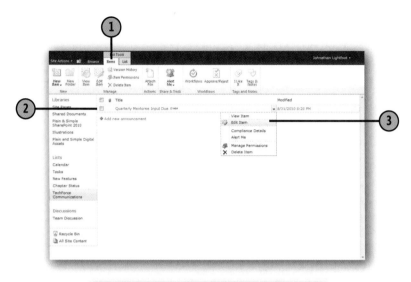

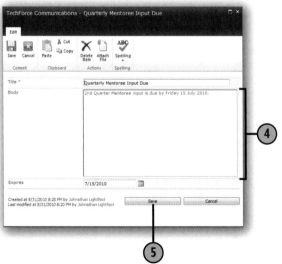

Delete an Item

① Click Items on the List Tools tab.

② Hover your mouse over the title of the item; and click the drop-down edit control block menu.

③ Click Delete Item.

④ Click OK.

Try This!

SharePoint lists support deleting multiple items in one operation. To delete multiple items, repeat the previous task, but select the check box next to multiple list items. To delete the selected items, use the ribbon.

Tip

Items deleted from a list are moved to a personal Recycle Bin and then to a site Recycle Bin that can be accessed by a site administrator. Deleted list items can be recovered from the Recycle Bin.

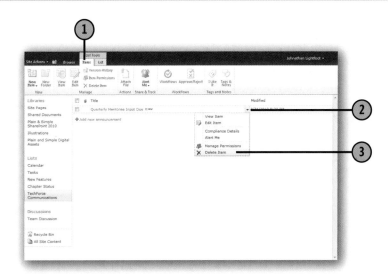

Organizing Items with Folders

SharePoint provides the ability for you to create folders in lists—in very much the same way that you create folders on your local computer. Research suggests that if you have more than 5,000 items in a list that you should employ the use of folders. However, we caution you to carefully consider whether to use folders in SharePoint 2010.

Chances are you are using SharePoint for the purpose of organizing information. As such, you might need a system in place in which you can find information as quickly as possible. For example, if you work for a security alarm company, you might have emergency contact information for each of the properties you monitor. You could have a list titled "Emergency Contacts," for example. Within this list you might set up folders for each of the properties and keep the emergency contact for each property in the folder. This is considered a good use of folders in SharePoint.

If you do not properly plan and implement your information management strategy, you could find yourself in the position of not being able to locate, manage, and process the information that you have.

Create a Folder

1. Click All Site Content.

(continued on next page)

Create a Folder *(continued)*

(2) Click the list or library that you want to create a folder in.

(3) Click the Documents tab on the Library Tools tab.

(4) Click New Folder on the ribbon.

(5) Enter a folder name.

(6) Click Save.

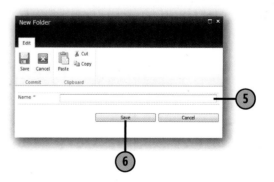

Working with List Columns

SharePoint provides a number of out-of-the-box templates for creating lists, including popular list types such as Announcements, Calendar, Contacts, and Tasks. Each of these list templates includes a predefined set of columns for storing data.

All SharePoint lists can be customized by adding new columns or—in some cases—by removing optional columns that were added by the template used to create the list. In this section we cover how to add new columns, edit column settings, and delete columns.

Create a Column

① Click All Site Content on the Quick Launch bar.

② Click the list or library that you want to work with.

③ Click List Settings (or Library Settings) on the List tab under List Tools.

(continued on next page)

Tip

You need permissions similar to the Designer or Full Control permission levels on the site to work with columns.

Try This!

Create a column that captures the anniversary date of a contact.

Create a Column *(continued)*

④ Click Create Column in the Columns section.

⑤ Enter a name for the column.

⑥ Select the type of information you want to store in the column.

⑦ Optionally, you can edit any of the additional column settings:

- Enter a description. The description is displayed on the edit form to help users enter column data.

- Select Yes or No under Require to specify whether this column must contain information. If you select Yes, users cannot save a new item without providing a column value.

- Select Yes or No to enforce unique values. Selecting Yes requires that the value entered for the column be unique for all items in the list.

⑧ Click OK.

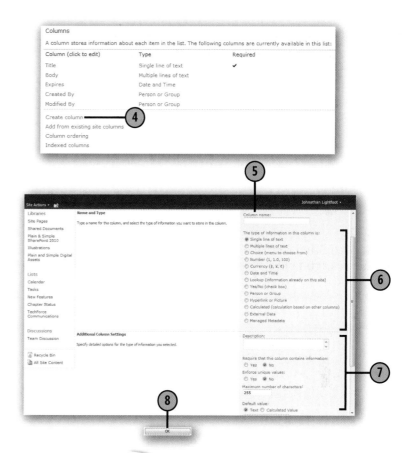

See Also

Column validation rules can be defined when you create a column or can be managed separately for all columns in a list. For more information on column validation, see "Using List and Column Validation Rules" on page 58.

Try This!

SharePoint includes a large number of predefined columns for storing types of information. Instead of creating a new column, you can choose to add from existing site columns when editing list column settings. Try adding an existing site column instead of creating a new column.

Edit Column Settings

① Click List Settings.

② Click a column title in the Columns section of the List Settings page.

③ Make any changes that you need.

④ Click OK.

Caution

You cannot change the column type after a column has been created. If you want the column to have a different column type, you must delete the existing column and then create a new column. This can result in the loss of any data stored in the column. Carefully consider the type of information you want to store.

Delete a List Column

① Click List Settings.

② Click a column title in the Columns section of the List Settings page.

③ Click Delete.

④ Click OK.

Tip

Some columns on lists cannot be deleted. The Title column included on most out-of-the-box SharePoint lists is an example. If the Delete button is not displayed when you're editing a column, the column is required in the list.

Tip

When you delete a column, all existing column data is lost. To back up the column data, try exporting the list to Excel before deleting the column.

Using List and Column Validation Rules

If you work with a team, chances are good that some of the information in your lists is incorrectly formatted or simply incorrect.

Lists in SharePoint 2010 include a feature called *validation rules*. With validation rules, SharePoint evaluates information that is entered in a list and uses the rules to accept or reject the information. If the information is rejected, the person entering the information has to correct the problem before the information is saved in the list. Validation rules exist on individual columns and also at the list level. When applying validation rules, SharePoint first evaluates column validation rules and then list-level rules.

Validation rules in SharePoint 2010 are set up very similar to those in Microsoft Excel, and they can be as simple or as complex as you need them. A detailed explanation of SharePoint validation rule syntax is beyond the scope of this book, but you can find a good reference in the SharePoint 2010 Help; just search for "formula."

Validation rules are not available on all columns and are only supported on the following types of columns: Single Line of Text, Choice, Number, Currency, and Date/Time. In this section, we cover how to add validation rules at the column and the list level.

Add a Validation Rule to a Column

① Click All Site Content on the Quick Launch bar.

② Click the list or library that you want to work with.

(continued on next page)

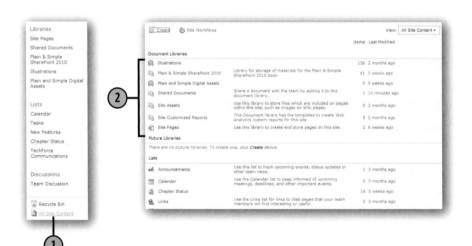

Add a Validation Rule to a
Column *(continued)*

③ Click Library Settings on the Library tab under Library Tools.

④ Click a column title in the Columns section. You might need to scroll down the page to see some columns.

⑤ Click the plus sign (+) icon next to Column Validation to expand the column validation options.

⑥ Enter a validation formula.

⑦ Enter a message to display to the user if the information entered is not valid.

⑧ Click OK.

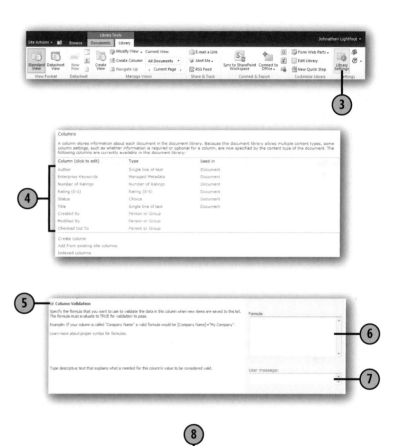

Add a Validation Rule to a List

① Click Library Settings.

② Click Validation Settings in the General Settings section.

③ Enter a formula.

④ Enter a message to display to the user if the information entered is not valid.

⑤ Click Save.

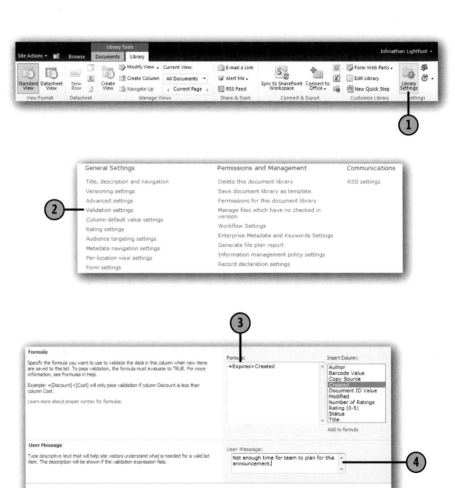

Sorting and Filtering Lists

List items are displayed to users through one or more views. Views can be created and configured to specify which fields are displayed, what order fields are displayed in, the sort order, and filtering and grouping options. Views can also be created to be displayed in various formats such as Standard and Datasheet views.

Standard views are displayed in a special grid control that supports dynamically changing sort and filter options using commands available in the column headers. In this section we cover using the Standard grid view control to dynamically change sort and filter options on a list view.

Sort a List

① Hover your mouse over the title of the column you want to sort.

② Click the drop-down menu icon.

③ From the menu, choose either Ascending or Descending.

Tip

Only a single column can be sorted by using the view header columns. To sort on multiple columns you need to configure a list view. See "Working with List Views" on page 63.

Tip

A small up or down arrow appears next to a column that has been sorted in ascending or descending order, respectively.

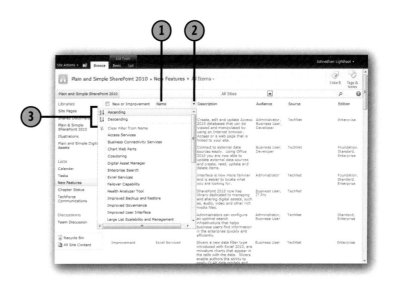

Filter a List

① Hover your mouse over the title of the column you want to filter.

② Click the drop-down menu icon.

③ From the menu, choose the Filter option. The list of filter values is automatically populated from the list column's contents.

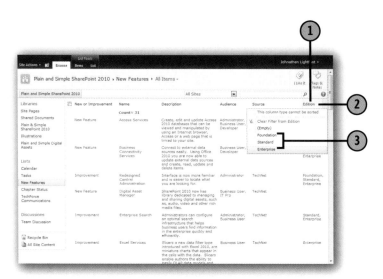

Tip

Filters can be applied to multiple columns. A small funnel icon appears next to any column that has been filtered.

Try This!

Clearing a filter from a column is accomplished in the same way you apply the filter. Just select the Clear Filter From option to remove a filter from a column.

Working with List Views

Views are a powerful element of SharePoint lists and provide a flexible way to create custom display forms for users interacting with list data. Views provide the ability for you to control which fields are displayed; the order in which fields appear in the list; and advanced multicolumn sorts and multicolumn filtering, including support for special tokens such as [Me] and [Today]. Views also support hierarchal grouping to create a treelike view of items.

Views support both personal and public views. Public views are displayed to all users who are viewing the list. Personal views are displayed only to the user who created them and allow users to create views that are specific to their needs.

Views can also be defined for mobile devices, allowing a customized list display for mobile browsers. A personal view can be created from a public view, but a public view cannot be created from a personal view.

Create a List View

1 Click All Site Content on the Quick Launch bar.

2 Click the list or library that you want to work with.

3 Click Create View on the List tab under List Tools.

(continued on next page)

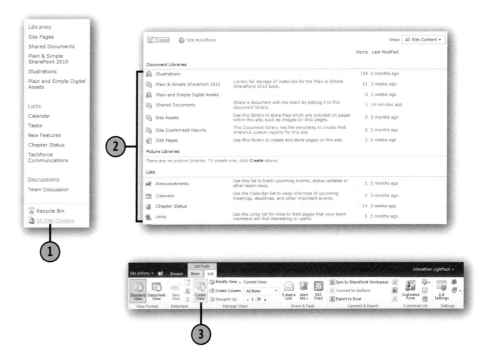

Create a List View *(continued)*

④ Click Standard View.

⑤ Enter a view name. The name must be unique to the list.

⑥ In the Audience section, select one of the available options:

- Create A Personal View creates a view that is only displayed for you.

- Create A Public View creates a view that other users can select and use.

⑦ In the Columns section, do any of the following:

- Click the check box under the Display column to show or hide a column in the view.

- Change the order in which columns are displayed in the view by selecting a position value from the drop-down list under Position From Left.

⑧ Click OK to save the view. (An OK button appears at the top and bottom of the page. You might need to scroll to see one.)

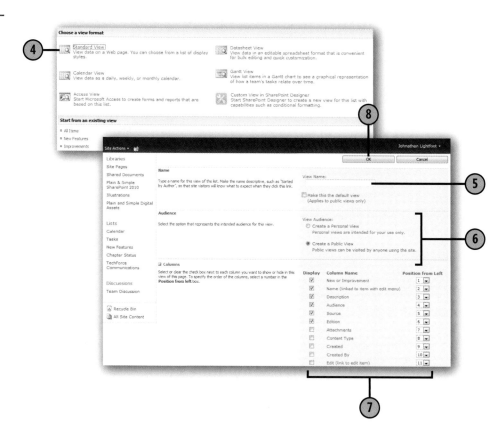

 Tip

To create public views, you need a permissions level equivalent to a site designer or owner.

 Try This!

Create a personal view that shows you the title and the Created By field. Name this view "My Limited View."

Tip

After you create a view, you are taken back to the list and your newly created view will be in effect for the list.

Select a List View

① Click the List tab under List Tools.

② Click the Current View drop-down menu.

③ Click the view you want to display.

Try This!

Select the last name in the breadcrumb trail. (It may say All Items.) You are presented with a list of choices for changing your view.

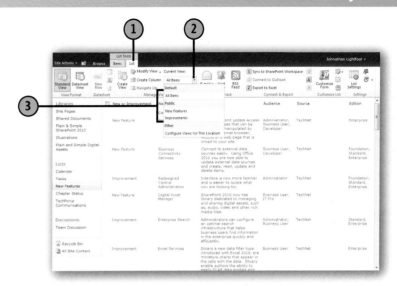

Sort a List View

① Click the List tab under List Tools.

② Click Modify View.

③ In the Sort section of the Edit View page, do any of the following:

- Click the drop-down menu for the First Sort and then select the column you want to sort on.

- Specify to show items in ascending or descending order.

④ Select the option to Sort Only By Specified Criteria if you do not want folders to appear before items.

⑤ Click OK. (You might need to scroll to the top or bottom of the page to see an OK button.)

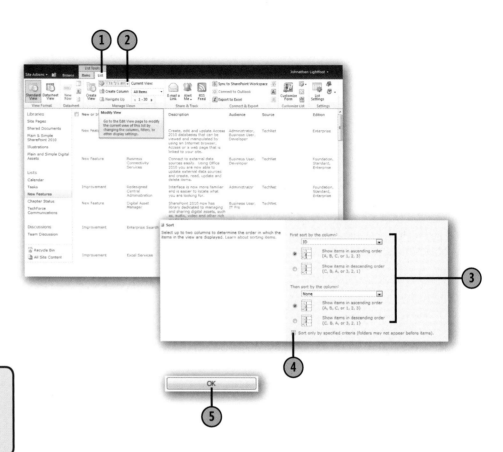

Tip ✓

By default, folders always appear before list items. If you select the Sort Only By Specified Criteria option, folders appear in the sort order within items.

Tip ✓

When you sort a list view, you set how this view is displayed each time the view is selected. This is unlike sorting a list, which always shows whatever the default view settings are when you open the list.

Filter a List View

(1) Click the List tab under List Tools.

(2) Click the drop-down arrow for Current View, and select a view to modify.

(3) Click Modify View.

(4) Click Show Items Only When The Following Is True to apply a filter to the view.

(5) Enter filter criteria by doing the following:

- Select a column to filter on from the first drop-down menu.

- Select an operation from the second drop-down menu.

- Enter a filter value.

(6) To enter additional filter criteria, select either And or Or.

(7) To filter on more than two fields, click Show More Columns.

(8) Click OK.

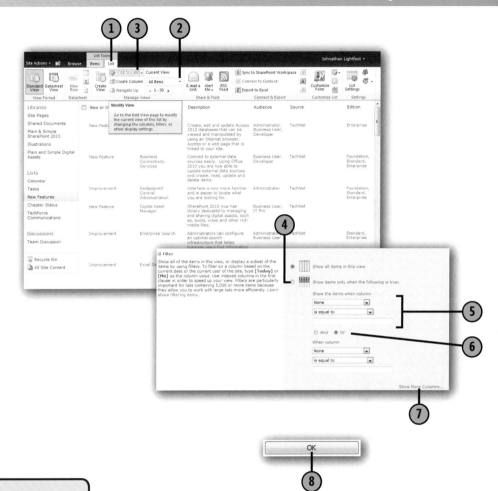

Tip

Filter criteria values can include special variables such as [Today] and [Me]. Use the [Me] variable to filter fields like Created By or Modified By or the Assigned To columns. The [Me] variable uses the account name for the current user viewing the list.

6

Working with Documents

In this section:

- Managing Documents with a Document Library
- Customizing Document Templates
- Uploading Multiple Documents
- Checking Documents In and Out
- Tracking Documents with Document IDs
- Using Send To Locations
- Introducing Document Sets

The origins of SharePoint were heavily focused on document management, and managing documents continues to be one of the key features that just about everyone who uses SharePoint takes advantage of.

In this section, we explain some of the most common ways to use document libraries and describe some of the features introduced in Microsoft SharePoint Server 2010, including the document ID server and document sets.

Managing Documents with a Document Library

The core difference between a SharePoint library and list is that a library is designed to manage files. A document library is a catch-all for storing just about any kind of document file.

A SharePoint site can contain many document libraries, and each document library can contain a hierarchy of folders and files. It is quite common to see many document libraries created in a SharePoint site for different types of documents, such as a library for sales proposals and another for contracts.

Create a Document Library

① Click More Options... on the Site Actions menu.

(continued on next page)

See Also

For more information about SharePoint list and libraries, see Section 5, "List and Library Essentials," starting on page 45.

Create a Document Library   *(continued)*

(2) Choose Library from the Filter By menu.

(3) Choose Content from the Filter By menu.

(4) Select Document Library.

(5) Enter a name for the document library, and then click Create.

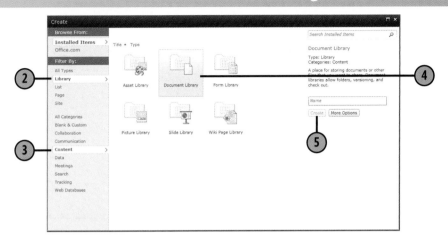

Customizing Document Templates

Document libraries come preconfigured with a Document content type and a default document template. When you create a document from the menu in SharePoint, an empty document is created from the template associated with the document library.

You can customize the document templates used by SharePoint in a number of ways, including customizing the default template for a specific document library or customizing the document template associated with a content type.

Modify the Document Template for a Document Library

① Open a document library from the Quick Launch bar or by clicking View All Site Content and selecting a document library.

② Click the Library tab under Library Tools on the ribbon.

③ Click Library Settings.

④ Click Advanced Settings in the General Settings group.

(continued on next page)

 **Tip**

The default document library can have only a single associated document type. If you need to have multiple document templates within a document library, you need to add additional content types.

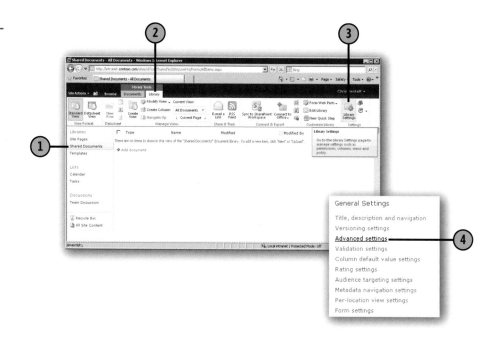

Modify the Document Template
for a Document Library *(continued)*

(5) Click Edit Template.

(6) Make your changes to the template.

(7) Save the template.

(8) Close the application.

(9) Click OK.

See Also

For more information on using multiple content types in a list or library, see "Managing Content Types" on page 35.

Caution

By changing the document library template, you affect how documents are created when the New button is clicked. You might want to experiment with a test document before performing these steps in a document library that your team is using.

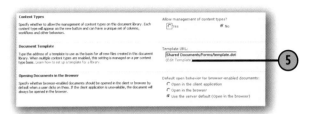

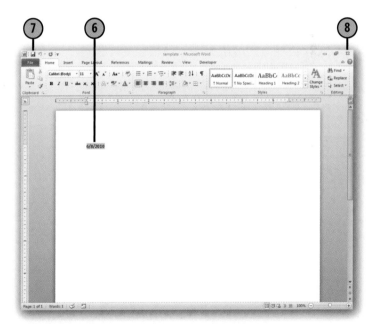

Modify the Document Template for a Content Type

① Click Site Settings on the Site Actions menu.

② Click Site Content Types on the Galleries menu.

③ Click Document under Document Content Types.

(continued on next page)

Caution

Changing an existing content type applies the change across an entire site collection. Consider creating and customizing a new content type.

Modify the Document Template
for a Content Type *(continued)*

(4) Click Advanced Settings.

(5) In the Document Template section, choose one of the following options:

- Enter The URL Of An Existing Template.

- Upload A New Document Template.

(6) Click OK.

See Also

For more information about using and customizing content types, see "Managing Content Types" on page 35.

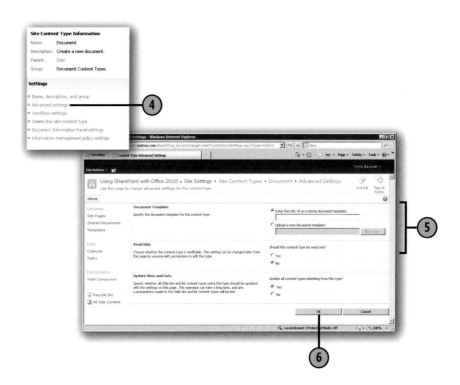

Uploading Multiple Documents

Anyone using SharePoint as a core platform for managing information is going to occasionally need to upload multiple documents. A frequent concern of new SharePoint users is how to migrate documents they currently store in other locations, such as local hard disks, USB drives, or network file shares.

SharePoint 2010 supports two convenient approaches to uploading multiple files: a browser interface in Internet Explorer that supports dragging and dropping and also integration with Windows Explorer.

Upload Multiple Files with Internet Explorer

① Select the Documents tab under Library Tools on the ribbon.

② Click Upload Multiple Documents on the Upload Document menu.

③ Drag files on your local computer to the Drag Files And Folders Here area. Note that you can drag entire folders or multiple individual files.

④ Click OK.

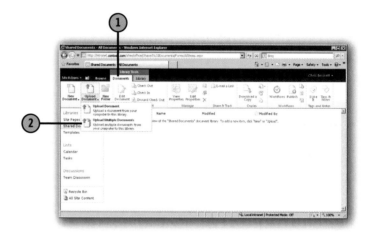

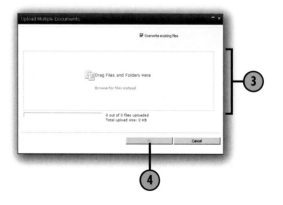

Upload Multiple Files with Windows Explorer

(1) Select the Library tab under Library Tools on the ribbon.

(2) Click Open With Explorer, and navigate to the folder that contains the files you want to upload.

(3) Drag files and folders from your folder location to Windows Explorer.

(4) Close the dialog box when you finish.

(5) Click Refresh in your browser.

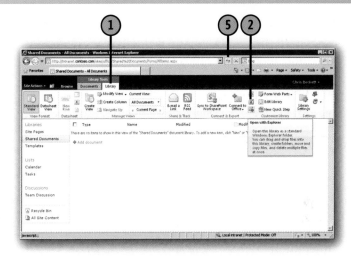

Checking Documents In and Out

SharePoint is a collaborative application that allows many users to store and share documents with others, and it is possible that multiple users might attempt to open and edit a document at the same time.

SharePoint 2010 lets you explicitly lock a document so that only one person can edit the document. Checking out a document places a lock on the document until it is checked in. While a document is checked out, changes to the document are not visible to other users who view the document. Changes can be seen by other people once a document is checked in.

Optionally, a comment can be added when a document is checked in and can be viewed in the document's history. Check out and check in can be configured so that it is required to edit a document.

Display the Check Out Status on a Document Library View

① Click the Library tab under Library Tools on the ribbon.

② Click Modify View.

③ Select Checked Out To.

④ Click OK.

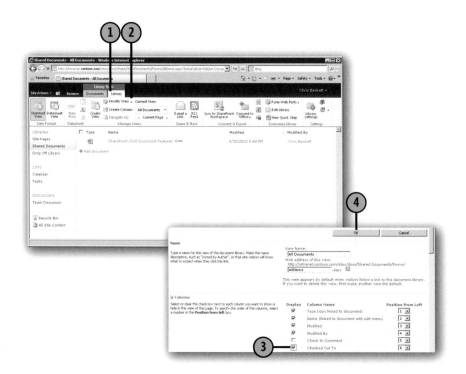

Check Out a Document

1. Click the check box next to one or more documents. (You have to hover the mouse pointer over an item before you can see the check box.)

2. Click the Documents tab under Library Tools on the ribbon.

3. Click Check Out.

4. Click OK.

Tip

When you check out a document, the icon changes so that it looks similar to this one.

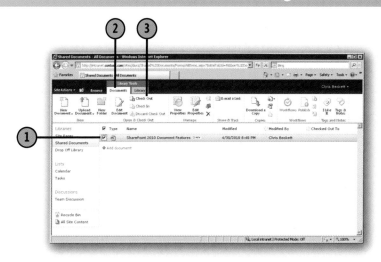

Check In a Document

① Click the check box next to one or more documents that display the green checked-out icon.

② Click the Documents tab under Library Tools on the ribbon.

③ Click Check In.

④ In the Check In dialog box, do any of the following:

- Select Yes or No to keep the file checked out or not.

- Enter any comments to include in the document's revision history.

⑤ Click OK.

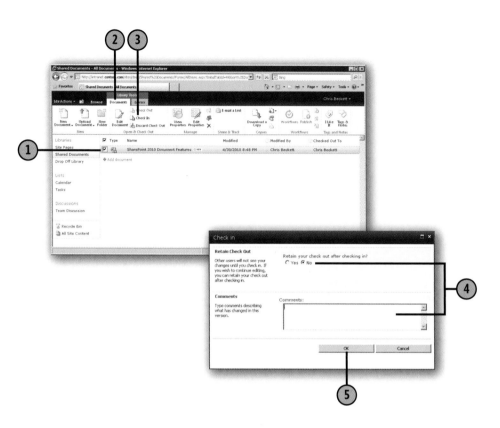

Require Document Check Out on a Library

① Click the Library tab under Library Tools on the ribbon.

② Click Library Settings.

③ Click Versioning Settings in the General Settings group.

④ Select Yes in the Require Check Out settings.

⑤ Click OK.

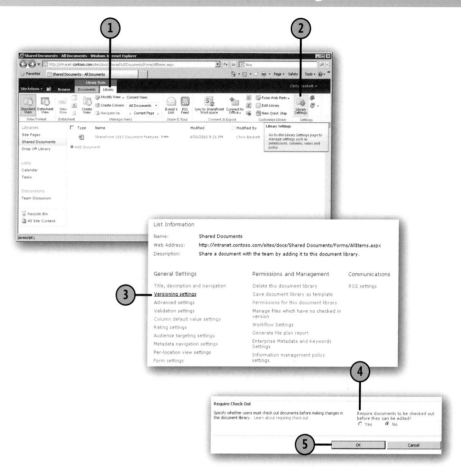

Tracking Documents with Document IDs

SharePoint 2010 introduces a feature called the document ID, which assigns a unique identifier to a document. A document ID is stored with the document as metadata and can be used to easily find the document anywhere in the site collection. A document ID is automatically generated and associated with a document when the document is added to a document library. A document ID can help correlate printed documents with an electronic copy and can also be useful for finding documents that have been moved.

SharePoint 2010 also includes a new Web Part that can be added to any page and used to find a document by its document ID. Adding this Web Part to your site's home page provides a convenient way for someone to find a document quickly.

Enable the Document ID Service

(1) Click Site Settings on the Site Actions menu.

(continued on next page)

See Also

To use the document ID service, the document ID feature must be enabled on the site collection.

Enable the Document ID
Service   *(continued)*

② Click Site Collection Features in the
Site Collection Administration group.

③ Click Activate next to Document ID
Service.

Tip

To enable the document ID service (or any service for that matter), you must be working in the top-level site of the site collection and have permissions to enable services.

Tip

After you enable document IDs, activation is completed by an automated process that SharePoint manages. You might not see the document IDs for some time, depending on the configuration of your SharePoint environment. You'll see a message that looks like this:

Configuration of the Document ID feature is scheduled to be completed by an automated process.

Configure Document ID Settings

① Click Site Settings on the Site Actions menu.

② Click Document ID Settings in the Site Collection Administration group.

③ On the Document ID settings page, do any of the following:

- Select Assign Document IDs to enable automatic generation of IDs.

- Edit the Begin IDs field to assign a new document ID prefix for the current site collection.

- Select Reset All Document IDs to apply the new prefix to existing documents in the site collection.

④ Click OK.

Locate the Document ID on a Document

① Open a document library from the quick navigation menu or by clicking View All Site Content and selecting a document library.

② Select a document by clicking the check box beside the document.

③ Click the Documents tab under Library Tools on the ribbon.

④ Click View Properties.

⑤ In the View dialog box, click the Document ID value to open the document. (Suggestion: Take note of this Document ID for use in the next section.)

⑥ Click Close to close the document dialog box.

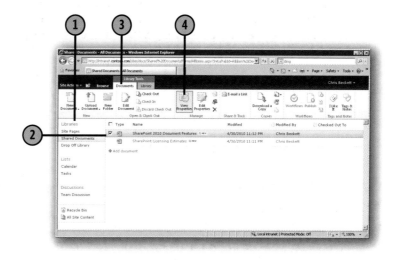

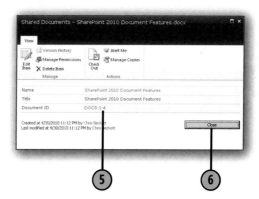

Use the Find By Document ID Web Part

① On the home page of your site, click the Page tab, and then click the Edit icon.

② Click Insert under Editing Tools.

③ Click Web Part.

④ Select Search in the Categories list.

⑤ Select Find By Document ID.

⑥ Click Add to insert the Web Part onto the page.

⑦ Click the Save & Close icon under the Page tab.

⑧ Enter a Document ID in the Find By Document ID field.

⑨ Click the Find icon to search for the document.

Using Send To Locations

The Send To menu can be used to copy or move documents between document libraries within or across sites and site collections.

Use the Send To Menu

(1) Select a document item by clicking the check box in the row header.

(2) Hover the mouse over the title, and click the drop-down menu.

(3) Click Send To.

(4) From the Send To menu, choose any of the following options:

- Click Other Location to move or copy the document to another library or site.

- Click E-mail A Link to open a new e-mail message in your default e-mail program with the URL to the document item embedded in the message.

- Click Create Document Workspace to create a collaboration site for that document. The document is automatically copied to the workspace.

- Click Download A Copy to download the file to your local computer.

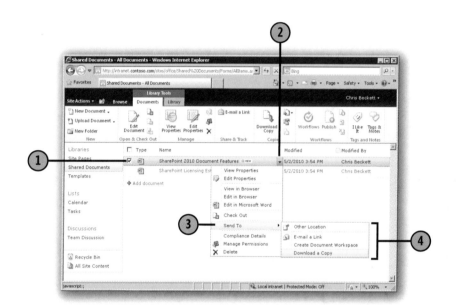

Tip

The default action when clicking a document is to open the document for viewing. The Download A Copy option on the Send To menu allows you to save a copy to your local computer.

Add a Custom Send To Location

① Click the Library tab under Library Tools on the ribbon.

② Click Library Settings.

③ Click Advanced Settings in the General Settings group.

④ Enter a destination name and a URL to a remote document library.

⑤ Click OK. (You might need to scroll to the bottom of the page.)

Tip

A custom Send To location can help aggregate official documents when a major version is reached or when a document becomes a record.

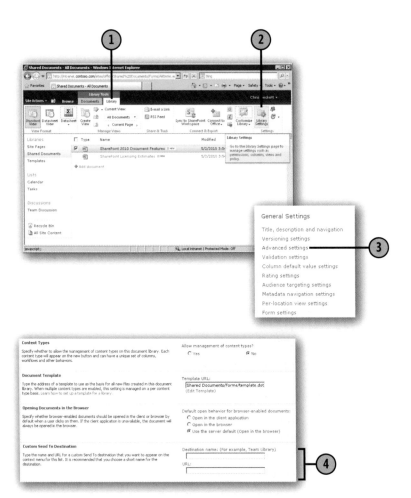

Introducing Document Sets

Document sets are a powerful new feature in SharePoint 2010 that allow multiple content items to be organized and managed together as a single item or work product. A simple example is a contract that has many addendums and other related files that need to be organized, tracked, and managed as a single content item.

Document sets are a bit like a folder on steroids. Some of the unique features of a document set include a Welcome page that shows metadata fields common to all documents in the set, a defined set of allowed content types, and even a collection of default documents that can be included in each new instance.

In this section we introduce you to using document sets, including how to enable the document set feature, configure a document library to support document sets, and create a new document set.

Enable the Document Sets Site Collection Feature

Document sets are an advanced feature and are not enabled by default on all SharePoint sites, including team sites. To support the use of document sets, a site collection feature must be activated to add the functionality to a site.

(1) Click Site Settings on the Site Actions menu.

(2) Click Site Collection Features in the Site Collection Administration group.

(3) Click Activate next to Document Sets.

Tip

To enable the document sets service (or any service for that matter) you must be working in the top-level site of the site collection and have permissions to enable services.

Configure Document Set Options

(1) Click Site Settings on the Site Actions menu.

(2) Click Site Content Types in the Galleries group.

(3) Click Document Set in the Document Set Content Types group.

(4) Click Document Set Settings.

(continued on next page)

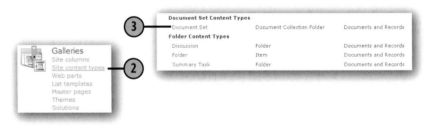

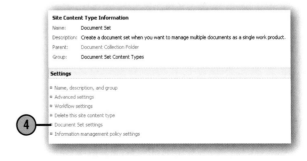

Configure Document Set
Options *(continued)*

(5) On the settings page, customize the document set by doing any of the following:

- Select a content type, and then click Add to allow documents of this type to be added to the document set.

- Select a content type and browse to associate a default file. When a document set is created, it automatically includes a copy of the default file. Click Add New Default Content to include additional default files.

- Select the Shared check box next to any content type property to share it across a document set. Changing the property value on the document set automatically applies the change to all documents the set contains.

- Select one or more columns to add to the Welcome page.

- Click Customize The Welcome Page to edit a Web Part Page associated with the content type.

(6) Click OK to save any changes.

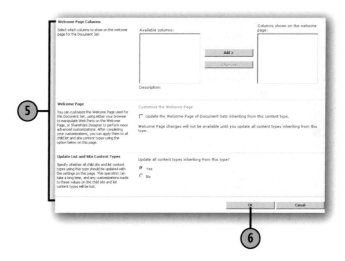

Enable Document Sets on a Document Library

(1) Click Library Settings on the Library tab (from any Document Library).

(2) Click Advanced Settings in the General Settings group.

(3) Click Yes for the Allow Management Of Content Types option.

(4) Click OK. (You might need to scroll down the page.)

(continued on next page)

Try This!

Create a custom content type from a document set and add it to a document library.

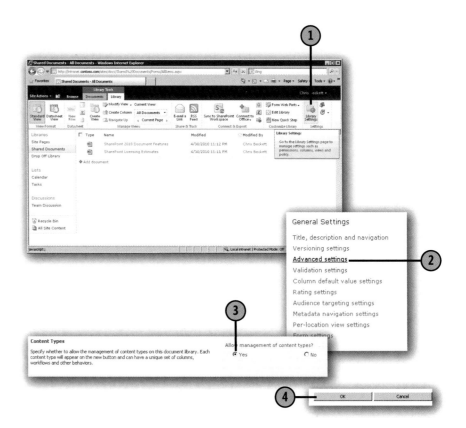

Enable Document Sets on a Document Library   *(continued)*

⑤ Click Add From Existing Site Content Types in the Content Types section.

⑥ Select Document Set in the Select Site Content Types From menu.

⑦ Click Add.

⑧ Click OK.

See Also

For more information about how to create custom content types, see "Managing Content Types" on page 35.

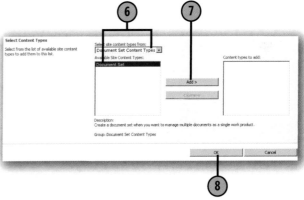

Create a Document Set

1. Click Documents on the Library tab under Library Tools.

2. Click Document Set on the New Document menu.

3. Enter a name and optional description.

4. Click OK.

Tip

Document sets behave like a normal folder when you add documents. Document sets can even be connected to Microsoft Outlook as folders to support drag-and-drop document management.

Try This!

On a document set Welcome page, edit and save a shared property. The property on each of the documents contained in the document set will be updated with the change.

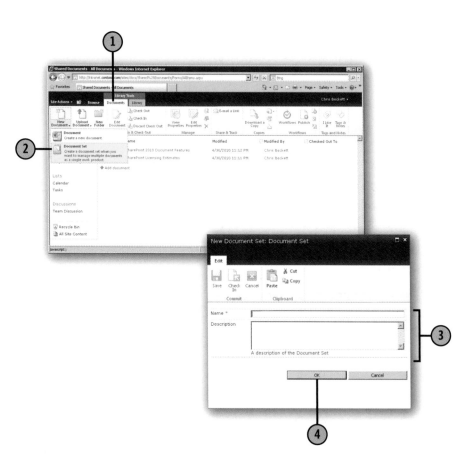

7

Working with Media

Video, audio, and image files have special significance when it comes to managing and storing content. Many of the common media file formats, such as JPG and MP3, support extended properties called *metadata* and involve special components for embedding and playing media on Web pages.

We touched on the concept of metadata in previous sections, but simply put, metadata contains information about content. Examples of metadata for an image file might be the date the picture was taken, the location as a label or GPS coordinates, exposure settings, and size. A popular term for metadata fields is *tags*. The key purpose of tags is to help organize and support searches based on metadata values.

In this section we show how to create and configure a new feature in SharePoint 2010—the SharePoint Asset Library. This library template provides a number of enhanced features for storing media files, including the ability to recognize metadata tags, promote them as columns, and allow navigation and filtering based on metadata values.

Getting Started with Media Sharing

SharePoint 2010 Server editions include content publishing features not found in SharePoint Foundation. These features provide enhanced functionality for working with media assets and for embedding images, video, and audio into Web pages.

To take advantage of these enhanced features, you must be using a SharePoint 2010 Server edition, and you must enable publishing features on your SharePoint site.

In this task, you will enable content publishing on a SharePoint team site so that you can work with the Asset Picker and the Media Player components later in this section.

Enable the Publishing Infrastructure Feature

1. Click Site Settings on the Site Actions menu.

2. Select Site Collection Features in the Site Collection Administration group.

3. Click Activate for the SharePoint Publishing Infrastructure feature.

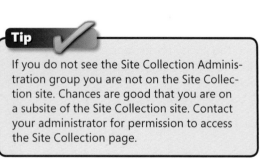

Tip

If you do not see the Site Collection Administration group you are not on the Site Collection site. Chances are good that you are on a subsite of the Site Collection site. Contact your administrator for permission to access the Site Collection page.

Enable the SharePoint Server Publishing Feature

(1) Click Site Settings on the Site Actions menu.

(2) Click Manage Site Features in the Site Actions group.

(3) Click Activate for the SharePoint Server Publishing feature.

Tip ✓

In this section, we discuss the Asset Picker and the Media Player. These components are part of the content publishing features that are available only in SharePoint 2010 Server editions.

Tip ✓

Creating lists and libraries in SharePoint requires elevated permissions on a site. For the tasks in this section, we assume that you have created or have access to a SharePoint site with the appropriate permissions to create and manage lists. All tasks start from your browser, with a standard SharePoint team site open.

See Also

For information about creating sites, see "Creating a SharePoint Site Based on a Template" on page 15.

Introducing the Asset Library

An asset library is a SharePoint 2010 library template that is optimized for storing digital assets—including audio, images, and video—and provides a thumbnail view of these media assets.

One of the unique features of an asset library is its ability to recognize the extended metadata information stored for media, such as Author, Date Taken, Tags, and Comments. The library also has the ability to generate and display a thumbnail image.

Create an Asset Library

1. Click More Options on the Site Actions menu.

2. In the Create dialog box, do any of the following:

   - Click Library or Content in the Filter By list.

   - Type **Asset** in the search box and click the search icon.

3. Click Asset Library.

4. Type a name for your library.

5. Click Create.

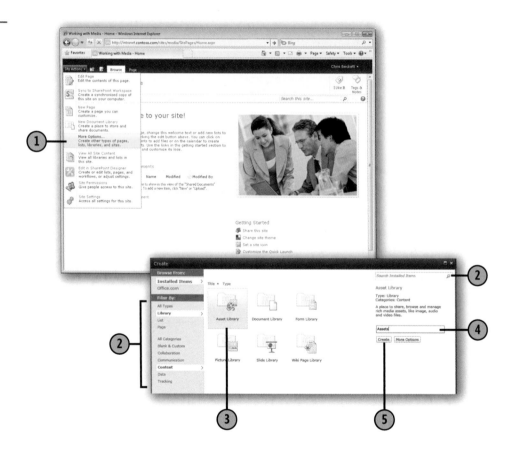

Organizing with Keywords and Metadata

Video, audio, and image files share common characteristics—for example, the standard file formats include metadata tags that can be used to help organize media files and make them easy to sort, filter, and search.

SharePoint 2010 includes a number of features that help extend the capabilities of an asset library. The Enterprise

Keywords capability supports recognizing and indexing keywords so that they can be used to organize and find media assets. Metadata Navigation provides tools to filter media content based on metadata tags.

In this task, we show how to customize an asset library to enable Enterprise Keywords and Metadata Navigation.

Enable Enterprise Keywords

① Click the Library tab under Library Tools on the ribbon.

② Click Library Settings.

③ Click Enterprise Metadata And Keywords Settings in the Permissions And Management Group.

④ Select the Add An Enterprise Keywords check box.

⑤ Click OK.

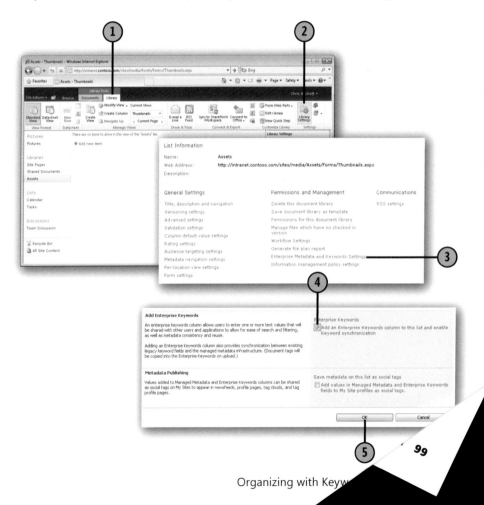

Organizing with Keyw

Enable Metadata Navigation

① Click the Library tab under Library Tools on the ribbon.

② Click Library Settings.

③ Click Metadata Navigation Settings in the General Settings group.

(continued on next page)

Tip

You must complete the task "Enable Enterprise Keywords" on page 99 to see the All Tags section.

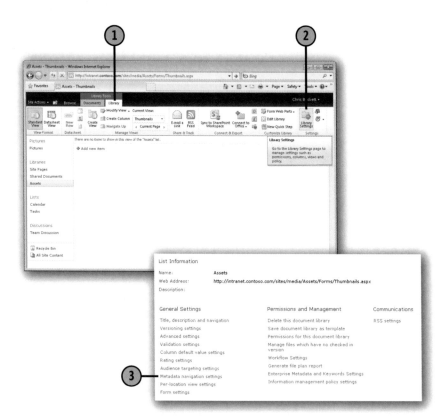

Enable Metadata
Navigation *(continued)*

④ Select All Tags in the Available Key Filter Fields list.

⑤ Click Add.

⑥ Click OK. (You might need to scroll to the bottom of the page.)

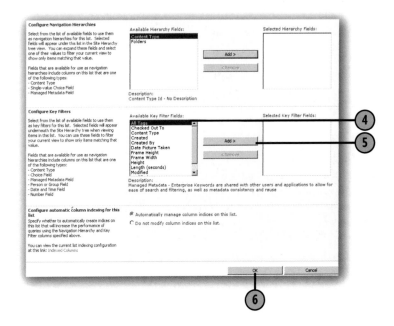

Tagging and Uploading Media Files

Many media applications let you edit tags and search on content, including tools such as Windows Live Photo Gallery, Windows Media Player, Adobe Photoshop, and Apple iTunes. Tagging support is also supported by the Windows operating system for picture, video, and audio folders.

A SharePoint 2010 asset library recognizes and preserves metadata tags on media files when the files are uploaded to the library.

In this task we show how to use the capabilities of the Windows operating system to tag images and then upload them to an asset library.

Tag Files with Windows Explorer

1. Open My Pictures or any folder on your computer that contains images.

2. If the Details pane is not displayed, select Details Pane from the Organize Layout menu.

3. Click to select any photo.

4. Click to edit any of the metadata items displayed in the Details pane for the selected media item.

5. Click Save.

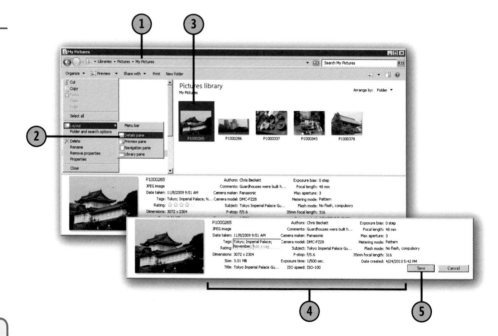

Try This!

The Details pane is a feature of the Windows 7 or Windows Vista operating systems. If the Details pane is not available, you can edit image properties by right-clicking the image, opening the Properties dialog box, and using the Details tab.

Tip

Some properties for image files are set by the device used to take the images and might not be editable. If you click a property and do not see an edit box, the property is read-only.

Upload Files to an Asset Library

① Click Add New Item on the asset library page.

② Click Browse to select a single image to upload.

③ Click Upload Multiple Files to upload a batch of files.

④ Drag photos from your local computer to the Upload dialog box.

⑤ Click OK.

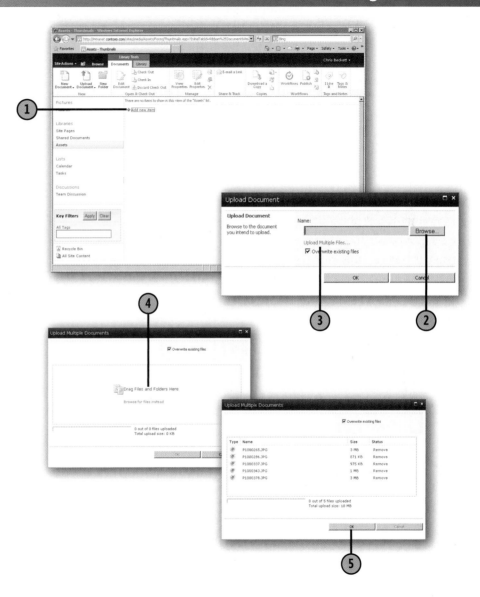

Using SharePoint Assets from Microsoft Office

The preparation of business documents is increasingly taking advantage of media assets in the form of charts, images, and even video. A common complaint at many organizations is that media assets are often locked away on the computer disks of individuals, which can make it difficult to find company media assets when you need them.

SharePoint 2010 provides tight integration with Microsoft Office 2010 so that media files stored in an asset library can be easily accessed and inserted into Office documents. This makes an asset library a powerful way to collect and share rich media across your organization.

Connect an Asset Library to Office

(1) Click the Library tab under Library Tools on the ribbon.

(2) Click Connect To Office.

Caution

After adding a SharePoint Quick Link connection to Office 2010, you might experience a delay of 5 to 10 minutes before it is displayed in the Office 2010 Open and Save dialog boxes.

See Also

For more information about integrating SharePoint Quick Links with Office 2010, see "Connecting SharePoint Libraries to Office" on page 144.

Insert Pictures or Video into PowerPoint

(1) Run Microsoft PowerPoint 2010, and either create a new presentation or open an existing one.

(2) In a content placeholder, do one of the following:

- Click the Insert Picture From File icon.

- Click the Insert Media Clip icon.

- Click Picture on the Insert tab on the ribbon.

- Click Video on the Insert tab on the ribbon.

(3) Click SharePoint Sites under Favorites in the Navigation pane.

(4) Click the Internet shortcut for the asset library you created earlier.

(5) Click any photo or video file.

(6) Click Insert.

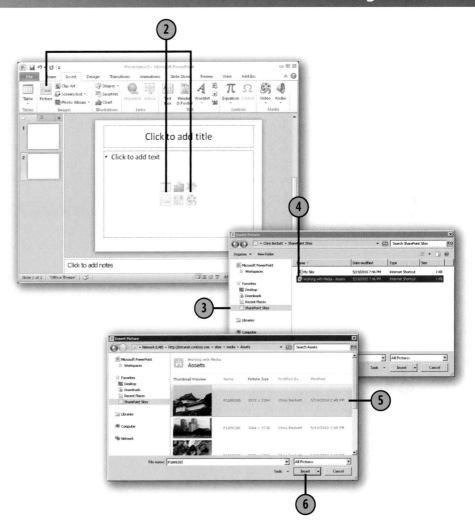

Adding Media to a SharePoint Page

All versions of SharePoint let you add images to a site page, but the publishing features in SharePoint 2010 Server include the Asset Picker dialog box, which makes it easier to browse and insert images, and the Media Web Part, which supports embedding video and audio in a page.

Insert a Picture from SharePoint

1. Click Edit Page on the Site Actions menu.

2. Click in a blank area of the page.

3. Click the Insert tab under Editing Tools on the ribbon.

4. Click From SharePoint on the Picture menu.

(continued on next page)

See Also

To enable the Media Player on the SharePoint ribbon, you must enable the SharePoint Publishing feature. For more information, see "Getting Started with Media Sharing" on page 96.

Insert a Picture from
SharePoint *(continued)*

⑤ Double-click the asset library that contains your images.

⑥ Double-click an image to insert it into the page.

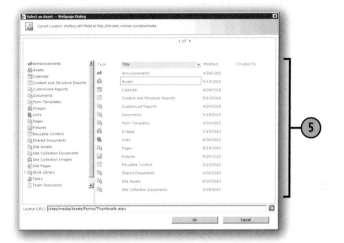

Insert a Video with the Media Web Part

(1) Click an empty area of a SharePoint site page.

(2) Click Insert under Editing Tools on the ribbon.

(3) Click Video And Audio.

(4) Click the Media Web Part. The Media tab is added to the ribbon.

(5) Click From SharePoint on the Change Media menu.

(continued on next page)

Tip ✓

SharePoint Server 2010 does not support live streaming of audio or video content.

Insert a Video with the Media Web Part *(continued)*

⑥ Double-click the asset library containing a video file.

⑦ Double-click the video file to insert it.

⑧ Click the Save icon.

8

Using Information Management Policies

We produce a lot more content these days than at any time in the past, which has made managing, tracking, and organizing information more diff icult. Out of the box, Microsoft SharePoint 2010 offers information management policies that can help you automate the management of your content.

Four information management policies are available to you: Auditing, Document barcodes, Document labels, and Expiration.

By using one or all of these policies, you can organize, track, and manage your content a lot more easily than before.

When you create your first information policy for a content type, list, or library, you need to specify a name and description for the policy. Afterward, you can write a brief policy statement (no more than 512 characters) that explains to your users that the policy is in place and what its purpose is.

Getting Started with Information Management Policies

An information management policy is a set of rules for a content type or the location where content is stored. Information management policy rules are called *policy features*. For example, an information management policy feature might require that a document barcode be applied to a document when the document is saved, or it might delineate how long a document should be retained before the document has to be reviewed for renewal or destruction.

Policy features are implemented on a SharePoint 2010 server by the SharePoint administrator for your organization; once policy features are implemented, site administrators can define policies. When Microsoft Office client applications (such as Word, Excel, OneNote, and PowerPoint) are used in conjunction with SharePoint 2010, policies are enforced on the server and in client applications, meaning that policy features are attached to a document and that policy-aware applications (such as those in Microsoft Office) prevent users from performing any task that violates the document's policy.

Using Auditing Policies

SharePoint 2010 provides a way to log events and activities performed by SharePoint 2010, by solutions, or by users working on content. This capability is referred to as *auditing*. Auditing is available for document libraries and lists, such as task lists, discussion groups, and calendars, and, of course, for individual items stored in either a list or library. The auditing feature can log the following events:

- Opening or downloading documents, viewing items in lists, viewing item properties
- Editing items
- Checking out or checking in items
- Moving or copying items to another location in the site
- Deleting or restoring items

Enable Auditing

1. Click the All Site Content link.
2. Click the list or library that you want to work with.
3. Click the List or Library tab on the ribbon.
4. Click the List Settings or Library Settings button located in the Settings group.
5. Click Information Management Policy Settings, located under the Permissions And Management section.
6. Click a content type that you want to audit.
7. Scroll down to the Auditing section, and select the Enable Auditing check box.
8. Select the events you want to audit.
9. Click OK.

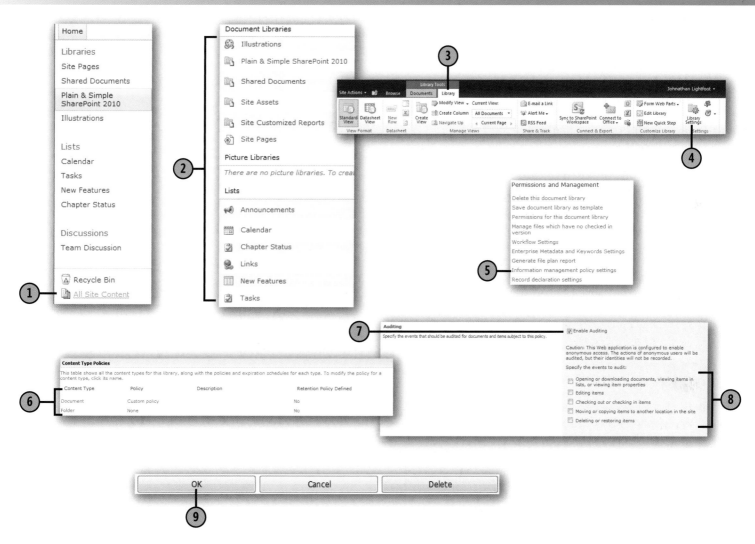

View an Audit Report

(1) Click Site Settings on the Site Actions menu.

(2) Click Audit Log Reports in the Site Collection Administration group.

(3) Click the type of report you want to view.

(continued on next page)

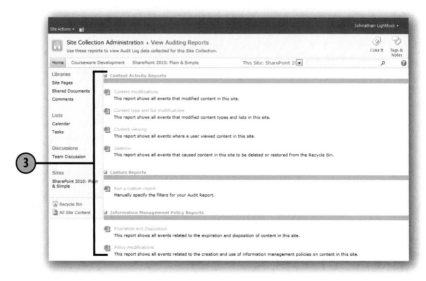

View an Audit Report *(continued)*

④ Click Browse.

⑤ Select the location where you want to store the report.

⑥ Click OK.

⑦ Click OK again on the Operation Completed Successfully message.

⑧ Click the option Click Here To View The Report. If no audit information is available, you receive an error message.

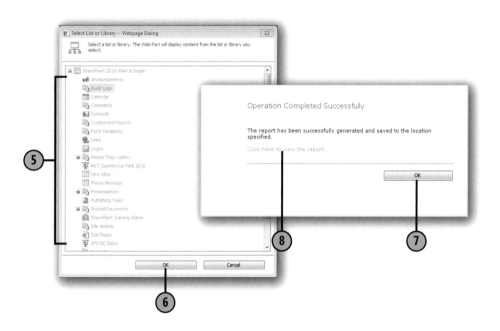

Tip ✓

To run an audit report, you need to have the appropriate permissions on the Site Collection site.

Tip ✓

You must be working on the Site Collection site to run an audit report. If you do not have access to this site, speak to your site collection administrator to arrange to receive the reports.

Adding a Document Label Policy

Another nice feature that SharePoint 2010 offers is the ability to produce text labels that can be attached to a physical or an electronic copy of a document. Document labels can be based on the content type's metadata, on static text that you provide, or on a combination of the two. For example, a purchasing department might want to attach a label that has the contract number, contract name, and assignment date to each of its contracts.

Enable Document Labels

1. Click the All Site Content link.

2. Click the library you want to work with.

3. Click the Library tab on the ribbon.

4. Click the Library Settings button in the Settings group.

(continued on next page)

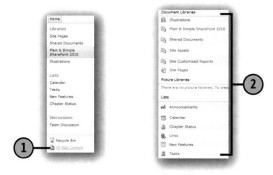

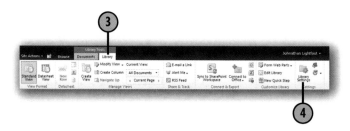

Enable Document Labels *(continued)*

⑤ Click Information Management Policy Settings, located under the Permissions And Management section.

⑥ Click the content type you want to produce a label for.

⑦ Select the Enable Labels check box. (You might have to scroll down to see the section.)

⑧ Select the options and formatting for the label.

⑨ Click OK.

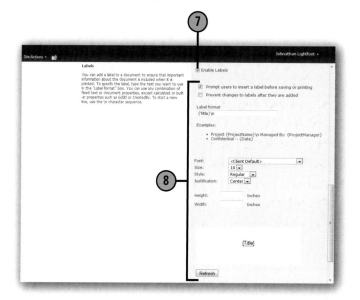

Tip

Click the Refresh button to update the information displayed in the preview window at the bottom of the Labels section.

Try This!

Create a document label that displays the document's title on a label 2-inches high by 4-inches long.

Insert a Label in a Document

① Click the All Site Content link on the Quick Launch bar.

② Select the library that has the document you want to work with.

③ Point to the document you want, and then click the arrow that appears.

④ Click Edit In Microsoft Program Name. (For example, Edit In Microsoft Word.)

(continued on next page)

Tip

The instructions for inserting a document label are based on using Microsoft Office 2010.

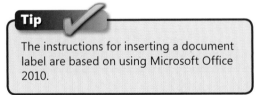

Insert a Label in a
Document *(continued)*

⑤ Place your cursor where you want to insert a document label.

⑥ On the Insert tab on the ribbon, click Label in the Barcode group.

⑦ Click the File tab.

⑧ Click Save.

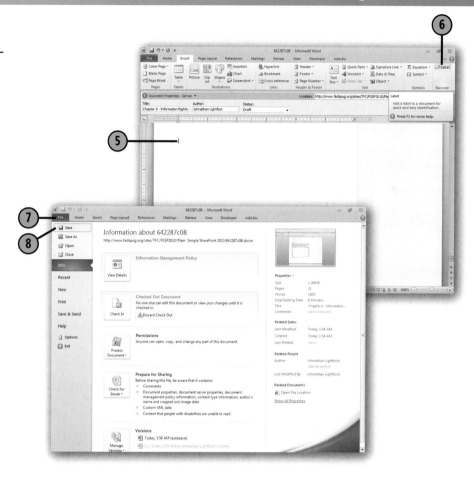

Working with a Document Barcode Policy

SharePoint 2010 also has a feature that lets you create and print document barcodes. Although similar to document labels, document barcodes are SharePoint 2010–generated unique IDs instead of text labels. Barcodes can be printed and attached to documents, or they can be inserted in an electronic file that is created in Microsoft Office 2010.

Enable Document Bar Codes

① Click the All Site Content link on the Quick Launch Bar.

② Click the list or library that you want to work with.

③ Click the List or Library tab.

④ Click the List Settings or Library Settings button in the Settings group.

(continued on next page)

Tip

Document bar codes in SharePoint 2010 are compliant with the common Code 39 standard (ANSI/AIM BCI-1995, Code 39). You can use other barcode providers if you have a plug-in supplied by them.

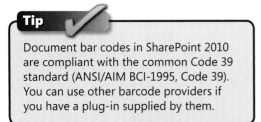

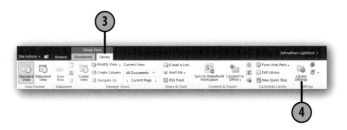

Enable Document Bar Codes *(continued)*

(5) Click Information Management Policy Settings, located under the Permissions And Management section.

(6) Click the content type you want to produce a barcode for.

(7) Select the Enable Barcodes check box. (You might have to scroll down to see the section.)

(8) Specify whether you want to require users to insert barcodes before saving or printing documents.

(9) Click OK.

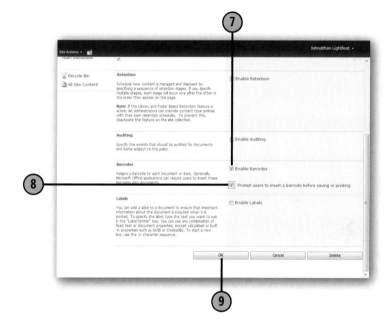

Insert a Barcode in a Document

① Click the All Site Content link on the Quick Launch Bar.

② Select the library that has the document you want to work with.

③ Point to the document you want, and click the arrow that appears.

④ Click Edit In Microsoft Program Name. (For example Edit In Microsoft Word.)

(continued on next page)

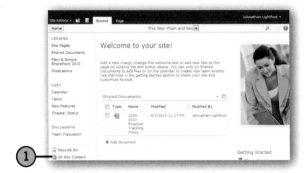

Insert a Barcode in a
Document *(continued)*

⑤ Place your cursor where you want to insert a barcode.

⑥ On the Insert tab on the ribbon, click Barcode in the Barcode group.

⑦ Click the File tab.

⑧ Click Save.

Tip

If you are using Microsoft Office 2007, click the Office Button instead of the File tab.

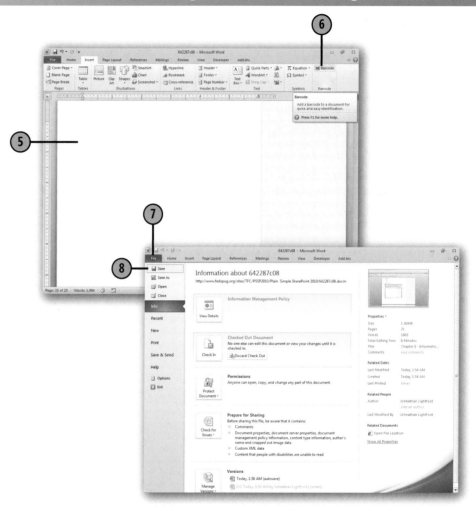

Setting an Expiration Policy

Just about all content has a life span, after which it is no longer relevant to an organization. Content in this state is referred to as being *expired*. After content has expired you can define its disposition. Here again you can align SharePoint 2010 and your business processes by using an expiration policy, which you can define using workflows with multiple stages. For example, you might have SharePoint send an e-mail notification to someone when content has expired because you want the person to review the content to see if it has any redeeming qualities. If not, a second stage can be started to delete the item. (For more information about workflows, see page 38.) If you define multiple stages, each stage occurs in the order defined on the Retention page.

A stage consists of an event and an action. An *event* is a trigger to activate a stage. This mechanism is based on a date property in the content's metadata that has a number of days, months, or years added to it. (The content's approval date plus two years, for example.) An *action* is the outcome you want to apply to the item. An action can either move the item to the Recycle Bin, permanently delete the item, transfer the item to another location (an archive location perhaps), start a workflow, skip to the next stage in a workflow, declare the item a record, delete previous drafts, or delete all previous versions.

This is another example of how SharePoint can adjust to your organization's business process for handling expired content.

Enable an Expiration Policy

1. Click the All Site Content link.

2. Click the list or library that you want to work with.

3. Click the List or Library tab.

4. Click the List Settings or Library Settings button in the Settings group.

5. Click Information Management Policy Settings, located under the Permissions And Management section.

(continued on next page)

Tip

The examples used here are for illustrative purposes. You can customize the formulas to match your needs.

Enable an Expiration Policy *(continued)*

(6) Click the content type to which you want to apply an expiration policy.

(7) Select the Enable Retention check box. (You might have to scroll down to see the section.)

(8) Click the Add A Retention Stage option.

(9) Click the date property you want to base the event on.

(10) Type the number of days, months, or years you want to use.

(11) Click Years, Months, or Days in the drop-down list.

(12) In the Action area, select the action that you want to invoke on the item.

(13) Click OK.

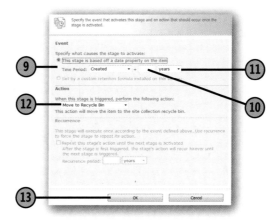

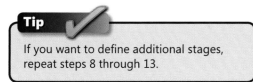

Tip ✓

If you want to define additional stages, repeat steps 8 through 13.

Organizing People and Work

Microsoft SharePoint 2010 provides a number of list templates that can help you track and manage people and work. A contacts list can help you track contact information for customers or partners. An issues list can help in tracking project risks, support incidents, or change requests for a product or service.

Many of these lists include special features specific to the type of list. A project tasks list can track dependencies between tasks and includes a Gantt view of task schedules. An events list includes a calendar view that can be used to track single or recurring meetings and can even provision a Meeting Workspace automatically.

SharePoint 2010 also has the capability to synchronize project tasks between a plan in Microsoft Project and a project tasks list, making it easier for project managers to get a bird's eye view of an entire project, while team members can focus on just the tasks assigned to them.

In this section we show you how to create and configure SharePoint lists that you can use for tracking people and work. To create lists in SharePoint you need elevated permissions on a site. For the tasks in this section, we assume that you have created or have access to a SharePoint site with the appropriate permissions to create and manage lists. For information about creating sites, see "Creating a SharePoint Site Based on a Template" on page 15.

Creating a Project Schedule with the Project Tasks List

Two core responsibilities of any project manager are to manage a project schedule and coordinate and track tasks across a project team. One of the most popular and universal approaches to handling this work is to use a Gantt chart, which combines a list of tasks with a calendar view.

SharePoint 2010 provides a special type of list called Project Tasks that combines the capabilities of a standard task list with a Gantt chart that displays task start and end dates and shows task progress based on the percentage-complete value of the task.

Create a Project Task List

1. Click More Options on the Site Actions menu.

2. In the Create dialog box, do either of the following:

   - Click List and/or Tracking in the Filter By list.

   - Type **Project Tasks** in the search box, and click the search icon.

3. Click Project Tasks.

4. Type a name for your list.

5. Click Create.

Add a Project Task

① Browse to the Project Tasks list. (See "Create a Project Task List" on page 128.)

② Click the Items tab under List Tools on the ribbon.

③ Choose Task from the New Item menu.

④ Enter task information.

⑤ Click Save.

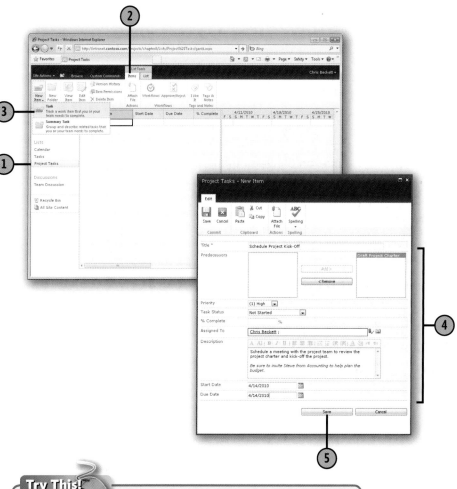

Tip ✓

If a task does not appear in the Gantt chart area of the Project Tasks view, the task start date and end dates have not yet been scheduled. For a task to appear on the Gantt chart, it must have an assigned date range.

Tip ✓

Predecessor tasks tie the completion of one task to the completion of a previous task. The Gantt chart displays lines with terminating arrows to show dependencies between tasks.

Try This! 🖱

A Summary Task allows you to group and manage related tasks in a folder. Try creating a Summary Task from the New Item menu, opening the Summary Task folder, and then adding tasks to the summary task.

Update Multiple Tasks with the Datasheet

① Click the List tab under List Tools on the ribbon.

② Click Datasheet View.

③ Click a cell to edit the value. Repeat this step to change the values of additional cells. Changes are saved automatically when you finish editing a cell.

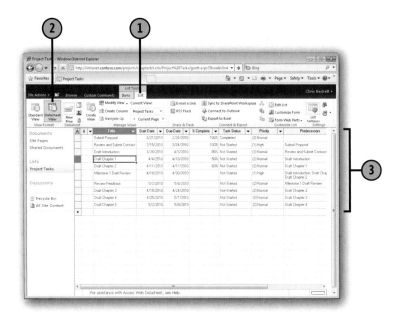

Tip ✓

The Standard view for a project tasks list splits the content display area between a datasheet and a Gantt chart, which are separated by a slider. Using the Datasheet view allows you to hide the Gantt chart to provide more room for editing task items.

Tip ✓

The Datasheet view includes a progress bar in the lower-right corner that shows activity when the datasheet is saving information to the server. On slower network connections you might receive a warning when you leave the Datasheet view if changes are still being saved.

Zoom the Gantt View

① Click the List tab under List Tools on the ribbon.

② Select a task row by clicking the row header column.

③ Click Scroll To Task.

④ Select either of the following to adjust the Gantt chart's scale:

- Zoom In to show a smaller time increment on the scale

- Zoom Out to show a larger time increment on the scale

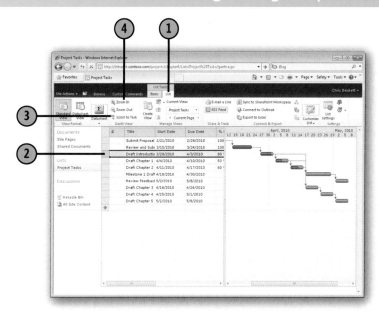

Tip

The Scroll To Task command brings a selected task into the Gantt chart view area.

Try This!

Drag the slider to the left or right to increase or decrease the display area of the Gantt chart.

Configure Task Columns

1 Choose Configure Columns from any column menu

2 In the Configure Columns dialog box, you can perform any of the following steps:

- Hide or display a column by selecting or clearing the check box next to the column name.

- Move a column up or down in the display order by selecting the column and clicking Move Up or Move Down.

- Change the display width of a column by updating the column width value

3 Click OK to save and apply your changes.

Scheduling Events with the Calendar List

A SharePoint 2010 calendar list provides a convenient way for everyone on a project team to keep track of important milestones, project meetings, and other events. A calendar list provides daily, weekly, and monthly views and provides many features similar to the calendar in Microsoft Outlook. Calendar lists can even be connected to Outlook and viewed side by side or overlaid with other calendars.

Create a Calendar List

① Click More Options on the Site Actions menu.

② In the Create dialog box, do either of the following:

- Click List and/or Tracking in the Filter By list.

- Type **Calendar** in the search box, and click the search icon

③ Click Calendar.

④ Type a name for your list.

⑤ Click Create.

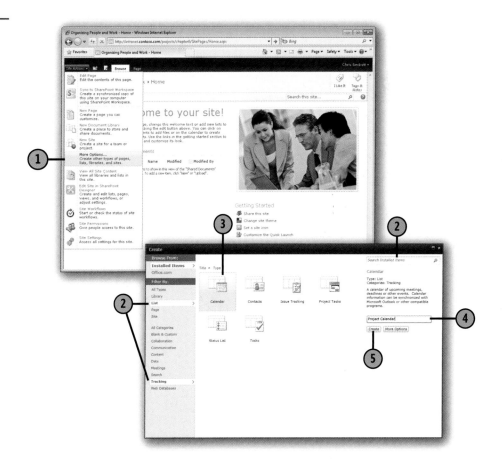

Switch Calendar Views

① Click the Calendar tab under Calendar Tools on the ribbon.

② In the Scope group, do any of the following to change the scope of the calendar view:

- Click Day to see events for a single day.

- Click Week to see events for an entire week.

- Click Month to see events for a calendar month.

Schedule a Meeting

1. Click the Calendar tab under Calendar Tools on the ribbon.

2. Click Day.

3. Select the date of the meeting from the mini-calendar.

4. On the Day view, drag from the start time to the end time to set the duration of the meeting.

5. Click Add.

6. Enter your meeting details.

7. Click Save to add the meeting to the calendar.

Tip

The Description field supports rich-text formatting. You can use the formatting toolbar to format titles and create bulleted and numbered lists.

Try This!

You can also schedule recurring meetings. Try creating a status meeting that recurs every week for five weeks by selecting Make This A Repeating Event when you create a calendar item.

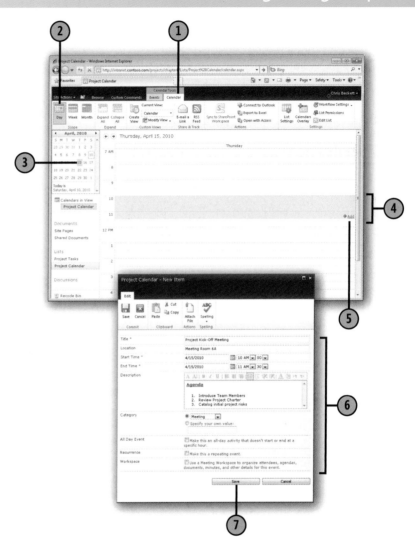

Using the Issues List

An issues list is a great tool that can be used for tracking many types of issues, including software defects, customer support calls, and project risks. Issue lists also let you track related issues and can be used to track activity through an append-only comments field.

Create an Issues List

① Click More Options on the Site Actions menu.

② In the Create dialog box, do either of the following:

- Click List and/or Tracking in the Filter By list.

- Type **Issue Tracking** in the search box, and click the search icon

③ Click Issue Tracking.

④ Type a name for your list.

⑤ Click Create.

Configure Issue Categories

(1) Click the List tab under List Tools on the ribbon.

(2) Click List Settings.

(3) Scroll down the List Settings page to locate the Columns section.

(4) Click the Category column to display column settings.

(5) Update the choice list to include the categories you want to track.

(6) Click OK to save your updated categories.

Tip

When you edit the category choices, the first item in the list becomes the default value for the column. Update this value if it is not the appropriate default.

Try This!

Any choice for a column in a list can be customized by using the procedure described in this task. Try repeating the steps in this task to also customize the choices for the Issue Status and Priority columns.

Enhancing Communication with the Discussion List

A discussion list provides the ability to track an initial request or comment, as well as all the replies to that post. This type of tracking is referred to as a *threaded conversation* or a *discussion*.

You can use multiple discussion lists to support the features of a typical forum, or you can customize a discussion list with a category column to track all discussions related to a specific topic.

Discussion lists can also be connected to Outlook and used to archive e-mail. The contents of e-mail messages are converted to posts, and messages that share the same subject line are automatically added as replies to the original post.

Create a Discussion List

1. Click More Options on the Site Actions menu.

2. In the Create dialog box, do either of the following:
   - Click List and/or Collaboration in the Filter By list.
   - Type **Issue Tracking** in the search box, and click the search icon.

3. Click Discussion Board.

4. Type a name for your list.

5. Click Create.

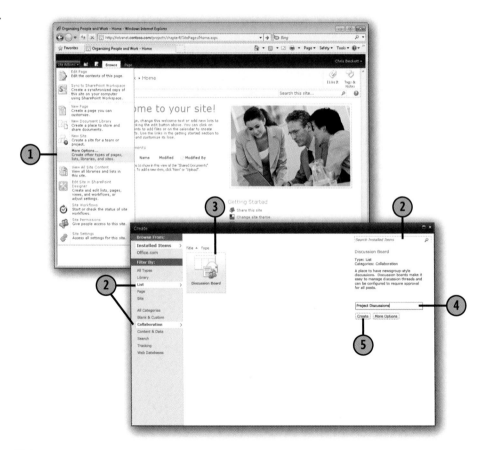

Start a Discussion Thread

1. Select your discussion list in the Quick Launch bar.

2. Click Add New Discussion.

3. Type a title and a body for the discussion item.

4. Use the Editing Tools tab to apply styles or insert objects into the body of your post.

5. Click Save.

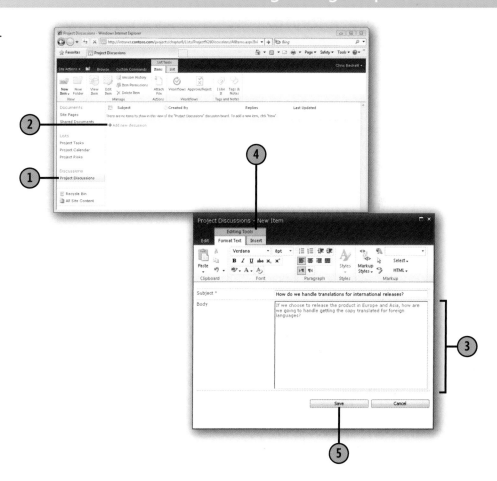

Reply to a Discussion Thread

① Click the Subject link.

② Click Reply.

③ Add your comments to the body of the item.

④ Click Save.

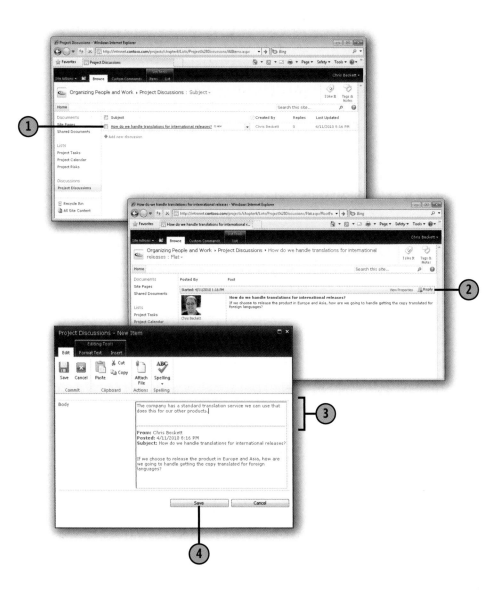

Synchronizing Project Tasks with Microsoft Project

Microsoft Project is a popular project management application that is part of the extended Microsoft Office family. It provides project managers advanced capabilities for managing and reporting on project schedules, resources, and budgets.

A common challenge of using Microsoft Project is keeping a project plan up to date with the task progress being accomplished across the team.

SharePoint 2010 and Microsoft Project 2010 now provide an integration feature that allows project schedules created in Project to be synchronized with SharePoint project tasks lists. Synchronization is two-way, allowing task progress to be updated in SharePoint and read back to the master Microsoft Project file.

The columns that are synchronized can be customized, allowing only some or all of the project task fields to be included.

There are a number of limitations concerning the integration to be aware of:

- Tasks in Microsoft Project must be manually scheduled. Auto-scheduled tasks are not supported, and tasks are flagged for manual scheduling whenever a synchronization is performed.

- Tasks in Microsoft Project that contain subtasks are represented as folders in SharePoint 2010 and are referred to as *summary task items*. Summary task items do not automatically roll up progress indicators of tasks contained within them. Summary task progress fields are updated whenever the project tasks list is synchronized with Microsoft Project.

To perform the following tasks, you must have Microsoft Project 2010 installed on your computer.

Sync with a Tasks List

1. Run Microsoft Project 2010.
2. Select Share from the File menu.
3. Click Sync With Tasks List.
4. Enter the URL to the site hosting your project tasks list.
5. Select Validate URL.
6. Select the Project Tasks list to synchronize this project plan with.
7. Click Sync.

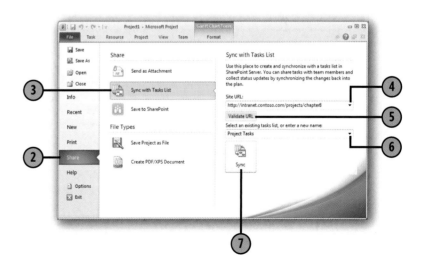

Manage Synchronization Fields

① Select Share from the File menu.

② Click Sync With Tasks List.

③ Click Manage Fields.

④ Click the Project Field column for any optional synchronization field. Fields that are disabled are required fields and cannot be managed.

⑤ Select a Project Field to synchronize with. Microsoft Project by default includes a number of Text fields (numbered Text1 through Text30) that can be used to map to columns in the project tasks list.

⑥ Click OK.

⑦ Click Sync to refresh the Microsoft Project columns in SharePoint.

Caution

The Save To SharePoint command requires Microsoft Project Server 2010, which is built on SharePoint 2010.

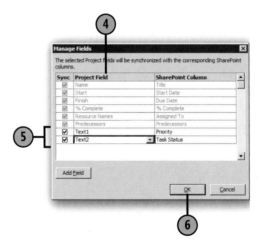

10

Using SharePoint with Office 2010

Microsoft SharePoint 2010 and Microsoft Office 2010 are core elements of a broader set of interoperating server platforms, desktop applications, and online services that make up the Microsoft Office system. They are designed to tightly integrate the personal desktop productivity experience of Office with the ability to share, collaborate, and manage information in SharePoint.

Microsoft Outlook 2010 lets you subscribe to individual SharePoint lists and libraries. Linked SharePoint folders support offline synchronization and provide a rich user experience for working with tasks, contacts, calendars, and other content.

Word, Excel, and PowerPoint let you open and save documents working directly with SharePoint document libraries, and also let you insert media assets that are stored in SharePoint. In addition, SharePoint includes special features for sharing PowerPoint content through its support for slide libraries and a new capability in the Office 2010 suite that lets you broadcast a presentation.

At the end of this section, you learn about a new desktop application called SharePoint Workspaces, which is included with Microsoft Office 2010 Professional Plus, Business, and Ultimate editions. Workspaces provide a desktop user experience for synchronizing entire SharePoint sites, and they support offline access and bidirectional synchronization of list and library content.

Connecting SharePoint Libraries to Office

SharePoint 2010 includes a personalization feature called Quick Links that allows you to publish bookmarks to SharePoint libraries to Office applications and share them between colleagues on your SharePoint My Site.

The Connect To Office feature in SharePoint appears on all library templates, including form, document, and asset libraries. A Quick Link provides a shortcut to a specific library location and appears in Office dialog boxes as a favorite under the heading SharePoint Sites. By selecting a SharePoint site link in Office, you can easily open and save content from Office without having to memorize or cut and paste the URLs for the SharePoint sites.

Add a Quick Link to a SharePoint Site

① Click Shared Documents on the Quick Launch bar.

② Click the Library tab under Library Tools on the ribbon.

③ Click Add To SharePoint Sites on the Connect To Office menu.

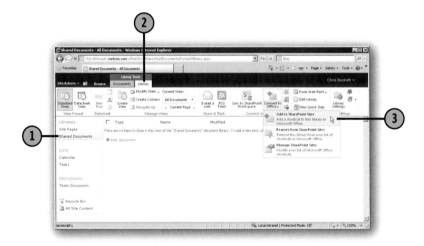

Try This!

SharePoint Site favorites are just hyperlinks, and they can be created within Office. Open the Open or Save dialog box, and enter the URL of your SharePoint site; Office then displays the site in the dialog box. Drag the icon adjacent to the URL in the address bar to your SharePoint Sites favorite's folder.

Caution

When you add a Quick Link to a SharePoint site, you often experience a delay of a few minutes before the link is displayed in the SharePoint Site favorites folder in Office.

Save a Document to a SharePoint Site

(1) Click Documents under Library Tools on the ribbon.

(2) Click New Document. If you are prompted to verify opening the document, click OK.

(3) Click Save & Send on the File tab.

(4) Click Save To SharePoint.

(5) Select your Quick Link in the Locations area.

(6) Click Save As.

(7) Enter a name for your document.

(8) Click Save.

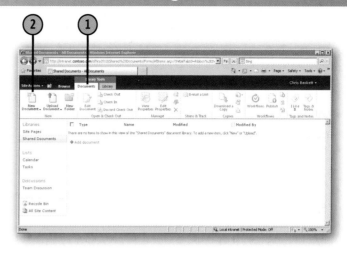

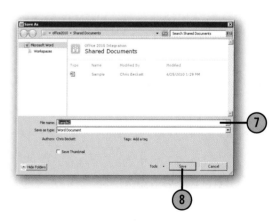

Manage SharePoint Site Quick Links

① Click Shared Documents on the Quick Launch bar.

② Click the Library tab under Library Tools on the ribbon.

③ Click Manage SharePoint Sites on the Connect To Office menu.

④ Select the check box next to a link.

⑤ On the Quick Links menu, do any of the following:

- Click Add Link to manually add the URL to a SharePoint location

- Click Edit Links to change the title of a link, organize links into groups, or change the privacy setting related to who can see the link on your My Site.

- Click Delete to delete the link permanently.

- Click Create Tag From Link to add the link to your Activity Stream and share it with colleagues in your organization.

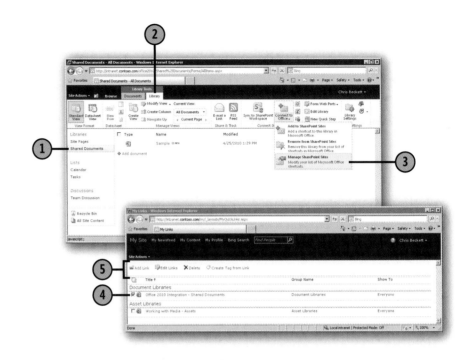

Try This!

SharePoint automatically includes a number of groups that it uses to organize links by the type of library (for example, Document Libraries and Asset Libraries). Try editing your links and organizing them in a custom group.

Connecting a SharePoint Calendar to Outlook

Like the Connect To Office feature covered in the previous task, the Connect To Outlook capability allows many SharePoint lists and libraries to be added as folders in Outlook. Lists and libraries connected to Outlook are available offline. When you reconnect your computer to the network, changes are automatically synchronized with SharePoint.

The lists and libraries that can be connected to Outlook include document libraries, contacts, tasks, calendars, and discussion lists. In this task, we show how to connect a SharePoint calendar list to Outlook and view calendar items in side-by-side and overlay modes.

Connect a Calendar List to Outlook

① Click Calendar in the Quick Launch bar in SharePoint.

② Hover your mouse over any date, and then click Add to insert a new calendar item.

③ Click the Calendar tab under Calendar Tools on the ribbon.

④ Click Connect To Outlook. If Outlook is not running, it starts automatically. The application focus switches to Outlook.

⑤ Click Yes to confirm that you want to connect the calendar to Outlook.

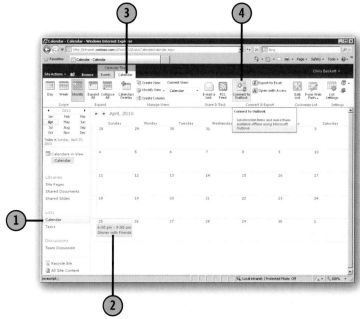

Try This!

Connecting lists to Outlook involves the same steps regardless of the type of SharePoint list or library. Repeat the steps in this task for some other lists, such as a task list, or with a document library.

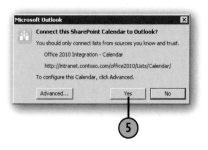

Copy or Move SharePoint Calendar Items to Outlook

1. Click Calendar on the Navigation pane in Outlook.

2. If the linked calendar you created in the previous procedure is not already selected, select it.

3. Right-click your SharePoint calendar item, and drag it to your Outlook calendar.

4. When you release the mouse button, you have three options:

   • Click Copy to copy the item to your Outlook calendar.

   • Click Move to move the item to your Outlook calendar.

   • Click Cancel to perform no action.

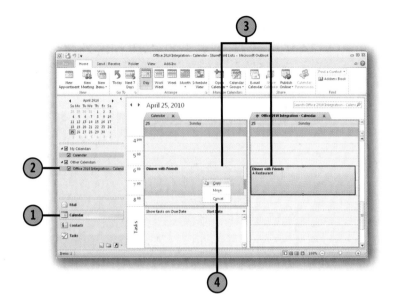

Tip

Calendars can be overlaid to provide a unified view of free/busy time.

Try This!

Items created or modified on a SharePoint linked calendar are synchronized with SharePoint. Create some new calendar items in Outlook using your linked Calendar, and then watch the changes appear in SharePoint.

Archiving Outlook E-Mail in SharePoint

E-mail was the first killer application on the Internet, and despite the rise of many alternative communication tools, it continues to be the prevalent way that business users communicate electronically, especially with external customers, vendors, and partners.

A common requirement of business users when they start using SharePoint is to store e-mail in SharePoint so that it can be shared with a team or preserved with other content from a project, contract, proposal, and so on.

SharePoint integrates e-mail archiving with Outlook by using a discussion list. The Discussion List template is designed to manage a threaded conversation based on a subject. When e-mail messages are moved from an Outlook Inbox to a linked SharePoint discussion list, the e-mail body is automatically aggregated into a discussion item as a series of replies. Attachments to any e-mail messages are preserved as attachments on the discussion list item.

Add Outlook E-Mail Messages to a Discussion List

1. Click the Team Discussion list in your SharePoint team site.

2. Connect the list to Outlook by using the steps shown in "Connect a Calendar List to Outlook" on page 147.

3. Click Mail on the Explorer menu in Outlook.

4. Select one or more e-mail messages in your Inbox.

5. Click Home on the ribbon.

6. Click your discussion list on the Move menu.

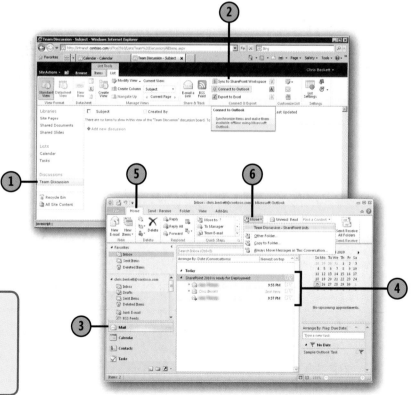

Try This!

Take any e-mail message and reply to yourself a number of times to create a set of messages with the same subject. Move the message items to the linked discussion list one at a time. Now review the discussion post and see how the messages were merged into a single discussion post.

Sharing PowerPoint Slides with a Slide Library

Business presentations created with Microsoft PowerPoint have become the workhorse of many business organizations. PowerPoint slides contain product strategies, marketing plans, sales forecasts, and just about every other type of business information.

Storing PowerPoint files in SharePoint is certainly a good way to share and collaborate on this valuable information, but have you ever wanted to just grab a few slides from another presentation when you were working on your own? Maybe to grab the sales forecast slide from the previous quarter to compare against the current quarter?

A SharePoint slide library is a special library template and provides a unique connection between SharePoint and PowerPoint that allows you to publish and share slides from any presentation. A slide library generates a thumbnail of each slide and tags slides with additional metadata from the PowerPoint document to make it easy to search for slides in SharePoint.

Create a Slide Library

1. Click All Site Content.

2. Click Create.

(continued on next page)

Create a Slide Library *(continued)*

(3) Select Library and then Content from the Filter By menu.

(4) Select Slide Library.

(5) Click Create.

(6) Complete the fields for the new library.

(7) Click Create.

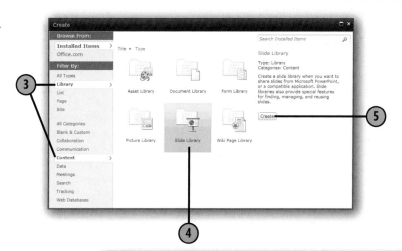

Tip

Slide libraries are similar to other SharePoint lists and libraries and can be configured to support custom metadata fields, content approval, workflows, and other standard features.

Try This!

Enable ratings on your slide library to allow people to vote for their favorite slides. You can do this if you enable ratings in the Document Library Settings section.

See Also

For more information on the capabilities of SharePoint lists and libraries, see Section 5, "List and Library Essentials," starting on page 45.

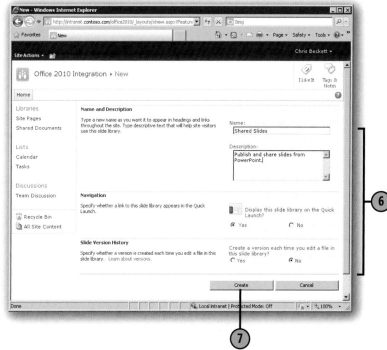

Publish Slides from PowerPoint

(1) Run PowerPoint and open a PowerPoint presentation. You can use one of the sample templates if you don't have a presentation file of your own.

(2) Click Save & Send on the File tab.

(3) Select Publish Slides from the Save & Send options list.

(4) Click Publish Slides. If prompted, save your file.

(5) In the Publish Slides dialog box, do either of the following:

- Click Select All to publish the entire presentation.

- Select the check box next to one or more slides in the preview area. You need to use the scrollbar to browse all the available slides.

(6) Choose a destination for your slides by taking any of the following steps:

- Enter the URL of your slide library in the Publish To field.

- Click the Browse button, and select a SharePoint site Quick Link.

- Open the Publish To menu to see a list of locations where slides have been published previously.

(7) Click Publish.

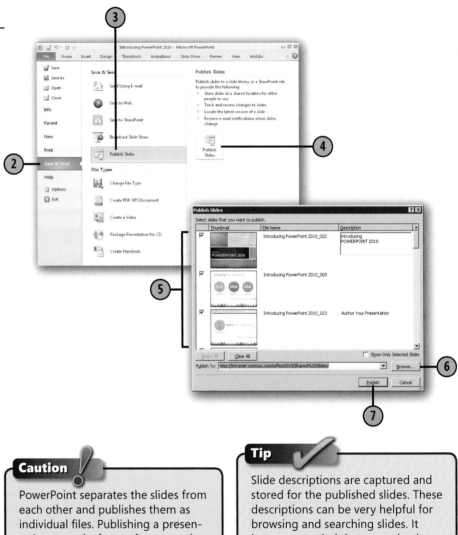

Caution

PowerPoint separates the slides from each other and publishes them as individual files. Publishing a presentation can take from a few seconds to a few minutes (or longer) depending on the size of the file.

Tip

Slide descriptions are captured and stored for the published slides. These descriptions can be very helpful for browsing and searching slides. It is recommended that you take the time to describe each of your slides prior to publishing them.

Copy Slides to a PowerPoint Presentation

(1) Click to open your slide library on the SharePoint Quick Launch bar.

(2) Select the check box next to one or more slides.

(3) Click Copy Slide To Presentation.

(4) In the Copy Slides To PowerPoint dialog box, you can do any of the following:

- Click Copy To A New Presentation to create a new presentation and insert the selected slides.

- Click Copy To An Open Presentation (if available) to insert the selected slides in a presentation you have open in PowerPoint.

- Select Keep The Source Presentation Format to preserve the original formatting on the slides being inserted. If you do not choose this option, the slides are modified to match the format of the target presentation.

- Select Tell Me When This Slide Changes to maintain a link between the slide in the presentation file and the original slide in the slide library. A visual indicator appears if the original slide changes.

(5) Click OK.

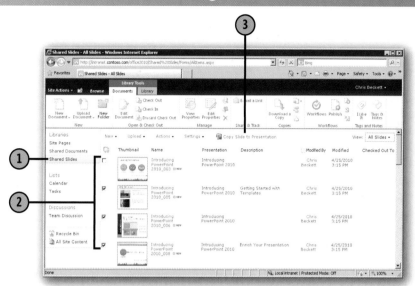

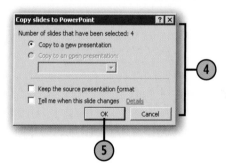

Caution

If you choose not to keep the source presentation format, there may be layout issues with slide content. Be sure to review the imported slides carefully to be sure that they fit your presentation theme.

Broadcasting a PowerPoint Presentation

Preparing and delivering business presentations with PowerPoint has become an essential skill for many knowledge workers. When PowerPoint was originally designed, it was assumed that presentations would be presented in person to a live audience. With the increase in global business and a mobile workforce, the need to make presentations to a remote audience over a corporate network or the Internet has become more commonplace.

SharePoint 2010 supports an optional set of capabilities called Office Web Apps that allow users to view and edit Office documents in a Web browser. Part of the Office Web Apps service is a new feature in PowerPoint 2010 called Broadcast Slide Show that allows you to present a slideshow across a network.

To make it easy for anyone to use this service, Microsoft hosts a version of the Office Web Apps on Windows Live. The use of this service is free to anyone with a Windows Live ID. Alternatively, your SharePoint administrator can install and configure a PowerPoint broadcast service locally on your corporate SharePoint site. The default location for this service is *http://<yoursite>/sites/broadcast*. You might need to check with your SharePoint administrator to verify the URL of your company broadcast site.

To get started with this task, run PowerPoint 2010 and open any PowerPoint presentation. There are a number of samples included with PowerPoint that you can use.

Broadcast a Slide Show

① Click the Slide Show tab on the ribbon.

② Click Broadcast Slide Show. Enter your Windows Live ID to log on if prompted.

(continued on next page)

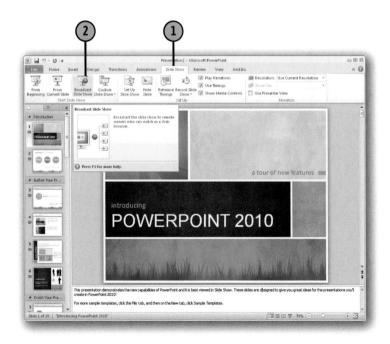

Broadcast a Slide Show *(continued)*

③ Click Start Broadcast.

④ In the Broadcast Slide Show dialog box, you can perform either of the following steps:

- Click Copy Link to copy the URL to the Clipboard and paste it into another program, like an instant messaging or chat program, to share the URL.

- Click Send In Email to open a new e-mail message with the embedded URL.

⑤ Click Start Slide Show, and then present your slides.

⑥ When your slideshow is over, click End Broadcast.

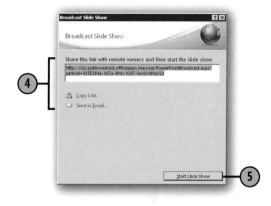

Tip

PowerPoint broadcasting does not support voice. To discuss a streaming presentation, you need to contact your audience by phone or another audio service.

Caution

Configuring a PowerPoint broadcast site on your company SharePoint site requires the help of your SharePoint administrator. Be sure to ask the administrator about this.

Importing and Exporting Lists to Excel

Spreadsheet programs like Microsoft Excel were one of the first programs written for personal computers, and they continue to be an extremely powerful and versatile business tool. SharePoint and Excel both contain features that make it easy to import and export data from SharePoint lists, including the ability to automatically map and create columns in SharePoint lists to match columns in Excel tables.

Excel tables can be linked to SharePoint lists by using a data connection so that data can be refreshed from SharePoint to keep data in Excel synchronized.

Import a Spreadsheet to SharePoint

1. In SharePoint, click More Options on the Site Actions menu.

2. Select List from the Filter By menu.

3. Select Blank & Custom from the Filter By menu.

4. Select Import Spreadsheet.

5. Click Create.

(continued on next page)

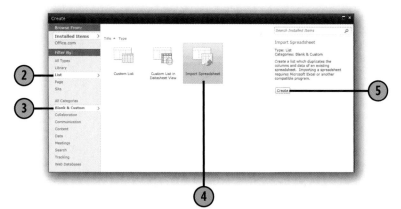

Import a Spreadsheet to SharePoint *(continued)*

(6) Enter a name and description for your new list.

(7) Click Browse, and select a spreadsheet file on your local computer.

(8) Click Import. If Excel is not already open on your computer, Excel starts, and the spreadsheet file you selected opens. The Import To Windows SharePoint Services List dialog box is displayed.

(9) In Excel, select a range type and range by using one of the following options:

- **Range Of Cells** Select a range by dragging your mouse across a selection of rows and columns in your workbook.

- **Table Range** Select a predefined, formatted table from the drop-down menu.

- **Named Range** Select a named range of cells from the drop-down menu.

(10) Click Import.

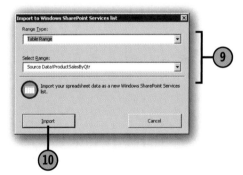

Tip

If you need to create a SharePoint list with a large number of columns, importing an Excel table into SharePoint can be a convenient way to create a new list quickly.

Caution

Excel is a very flexible program with some advanced data layout features, including the ability to merge cells. SharePoint can only import tabular formatted data into lists.

Export a List to Excel from SharePoint

1. Click List under the List Tools tab on the ribbon.

2. Click Export To Excel.

3. Select Open. Excel opens automatically.

4. Click Enable at the security prompt.

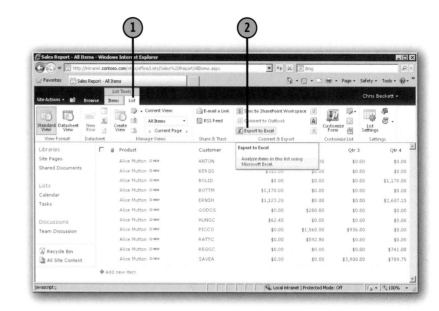

Exporting a list to Excel creates a new data connection that provides a number of options, including the ability to automatically refresh the data every time the workbook is opened. Review the data connections in Excel to further customize this feature.

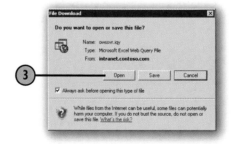

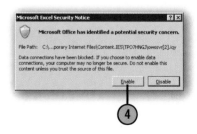

Export a Table from Excel to SharePoint

① Open Excel, and insert or select a formatted table. Excel can only export data in table format to SharePoint.

② Click the Design tab under Table Tools on the ribbon.

③ Click Export Table to SharePoint List on the Export menu.

④ To specify the address to publish to, do either of the following:

- Type the URL to a SharePoint site.

- Select a Quick Link from the dropdown list of sites that were previously published to.

⑤ Enter a name and optional description for the new SharePoint list.

⑥ Click Next.

⑦ Click Finish.

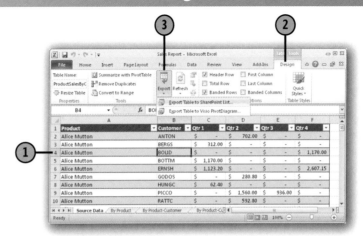

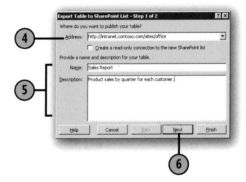

Tip ✓

To keep the table data in Excel synchronized with SharePoint, select the option to create a read-only data connection. This allows you to refresh the data in Excel to retrieve the most up-to-date information.

See Also ▸

For bidirectional synchronization of data, you can link lists to Access or use a SharePoint workspace. For more information see the next section, "Connecting Access and SharePoint," or "Sync to SharePoint Workspace" on page 162.

Connecting Access and SharePoint

The SharePoint Datasheet view is based on Access technologies, and Access provides a powerful tool for interacting with SharePoint data in either table format or as part of a custom business application. Access provides bidirectional synchronization of data when you use a linked table.

Opening a SharePoint List in Access

① Click the List tab under List Tools on the ribbon.

② Click Open With Access.

③ Click Browse to select an existing or a new database.

④ Choose from two options to export the list:

- Link To Data On The SharePoint Site to create a table linked to SharePoint that will always reflect the latest changes in SharePoint.

- Export A Copy Of The Data to an Access table. No further synchronization is performed.

⑤ Click OK.

Introducing SharePoint Workspace

Microsoft SharePoint Workspace 2010 (formerly known as Microsoft Office Groove 2007) has been revamped and rebranded to reflect its new focus—to provide a rich desktop experience for interacting with SharePoint sites. SharePoint Workspace is included in Microsoft Office Professional Plus and includes offline capability and bidirectional synchronization.

Create a Workspace Account

① Start SharePoint Workspace 2010 from the Start menu under All Programs > SharePoint 2010.

② Select Create A New Account.

③ Click Next.

④ Select Create The Account Using Your E-Mail Address.

⑤ Enter your name and e-mail address.

⑥ Click Finish.

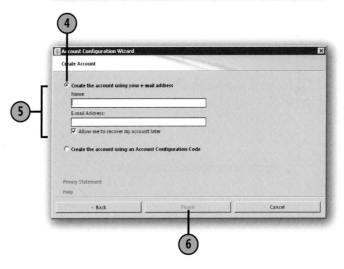

Sync to SharePoint Workspace

(1) Click Sync To SharePoint Workspace on the Site Actions menu.

(2) Click Configure.

(3) Click a supported list or library.

(4) Click the Download drop-down list, and select a synchronization option.

(5) Click OK.

(6) Close the dialog box by choosing either of the following options:

- Open Workspace opens the new workspace on your desktop.

- Close returns you to your browser.

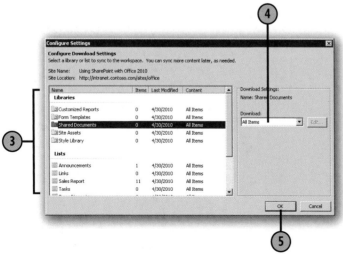

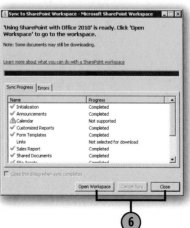

Collaborating with Blogs

A *Web Log*, more commonly referred to by the abbreviation *blog*, is used to publish and share short articles called *posts*. The author of a blog post is referred to as a *blogger*, and the act of creating and publishing entries is called *blogging*. Blogs are characterized by their format and style: a frequent series of short posts written in an informal tone and displayed in reverse chronological (most recent first) order.

A blog can be used for both personal and business purposes and can share information on any number of topics. Personal blogs are commonly used as an online diary of events and observations for a network of friends and family. Within corporations, blogging for business purposes is becoming increasingly popular as organizations realize the potential to capture knowledge, increase internal collaboration, and build stronger relationships with important target groups, such as customers, investors, and partners.

Microsoft SharePoint 2010 includes a full-featured Blog Site template with all the essential bells and whistles to enhance ad hoc collaboration with your peers, share knowledge across company projects, or publish news and updates for an entire department.

In this section we show you how to get started with your own blog on SharePoint 2010, including important skills you use for organizing posts and managing comments.

What's Where in a Blog Site

A blog site is defined by how it presents content to users—a series of blog posts in reverse chronological order (most recent entries first). SharePoint 2010 blog sites also include information about the author and the purpose or description of the site. Additional features include the ability to filter posts by category or calendar month, bookmark or share a link to a post, and subscribe to the blog using any RSS reader client.

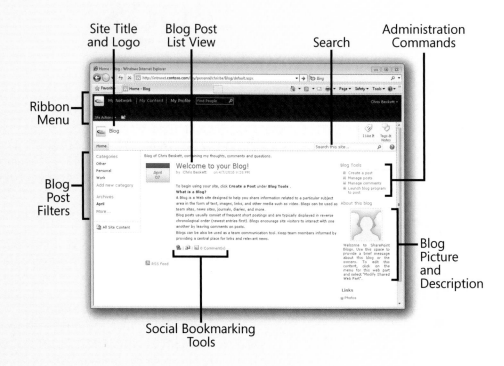

Site Title and Logo

Blog Post List View

Search

Administration Commands

Ribbon Menu

Blog Post Filters

Social Bookmarking Tools

Blog Picture and Description

Creating a Blog Site

You create a blog site in SharePoint by creating a new site or site collection and selecting the Blog Site template. In many cases, creating a blog site might be a task you request from the SharePoint administrator at your workplace. In organizations that run the SharePoint 2010 Standard or Enterprise edition and have enabled personal sites, you can create a blog site that's associated with your profile (also known as your *My Site*).

Create a Blog Site from Your SharePoint Profile

① On any SharePoint site, click the Personal Navigation menu.

② Click My Profile.

③ Click the Content tab.

④ Click the Create Blog link to create your personal blog site.

Caution

If the Create Blog link is not displayed on the Content tab of your profile page, your organization might not allow personal blogging sites. Check with your company's SharePoint administrator or human resources department for more information about the corporate policy related to blogging.

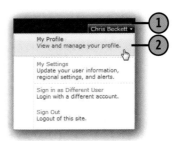

Change Your Blog Picture and Description

Once you have a new blog site, you will want to customize and configure the site before you start writing posts. Your new blog includes an About This Blog area where you can insert a picture or an avatar and include some text for readers, letting them know who you are and what you plan to write about. You might also decide to add or change the default categories that can be used to organize your blog posts by topics.

Change Your Blog Picture

① Click the drop-down arrow in the About This Blog title bar.

② Click Edit Web Part.

③ Click the placeholder image.

④ Select the Design tab under Picture Tools on the ribbon.

⑤ Click the Change Picture command.

⑥ Click From Computer.

(continued on next page)

Tip

You can resize your blog picture by grabbing the handles that appear when you select the image with your mouse and then dragging the mouse while pressing the left mouse button.

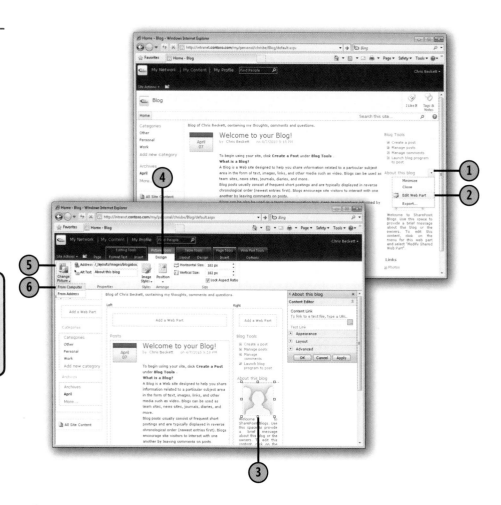

Change Your Blog Picture *(continued)*

(7) Click the Browse button, and select a picture from your local computer to upload.

(8) Click Open.

(9) Click OK.

(10) In the Photos pop-up, you can add descriptive information about your photo.

(11) Click Save.

Try This!

In "Editing Your User Profile" on page 199, you learn how to upload a personal photo that is stored in your Shared Documents library. If you have a user profile and you want to use the same photo on your blog, try changing your blog picture, but use the URL to the photo saved in Shared Documents. If you change your user profile photo, the image on your blog changes automatically as well.

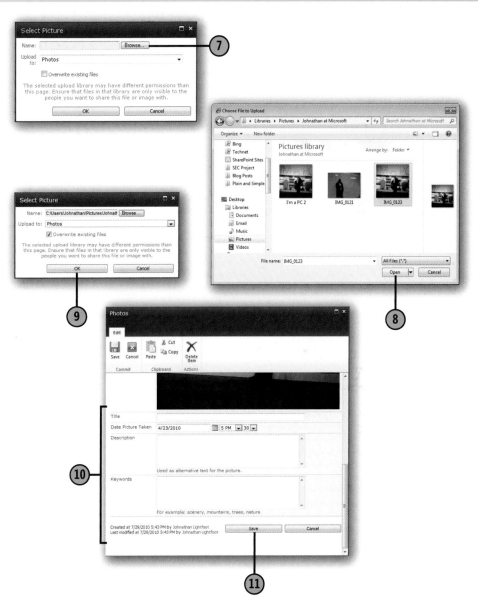

Edit Your Blog Description

① Click and drag your mouse over the placeholder to highlight the entire block of text, and type a new description.

② Click Format Text under Editing Tools on the ribbon.

③ Click Markup Styles.

④ Click Colored Heading 4.

⑤ Click OK.

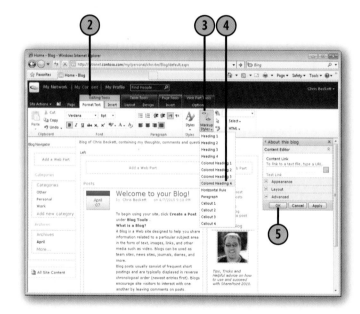

Using Categories

Categories help authors organize their content, and they help visitors find information they are most interested in. Although using categories to help manage your blog is not required, most bloggers find them beneficial. You can use categories to separate personal and professional posts or to organize your blog posts by specific subjects or topics. Your SharePoint blog site comes configured with three categories: Other, Personal, and Business. You can replace or add to these categories at any time, and a blog post can be tagged with none, one, or many categories.

Create a New Category

(1) Click Add New Category.

(2) Enter the title for your category.

(3) Click Save.

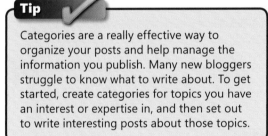

Tip

Categories are a really effective way to organize your posts and help manage the information you publish. Many new bloggers struggle to know what to write about. To get started, create categories for topics you have an interest or expertise in, and then set out to write interesting posts about those topics.

Edit a Category

① Click the Categories link on the Quick Launch bar.

② Click the Edit icon to the right of one of your categories.

③ Enter a new title for the category.

④ Click Save.

Try This!

You can also delete a category by selecting the Delete Item command. Use caution, however; if you delete a category that you used to tag existing blog posts, the category is removed from all these posts.

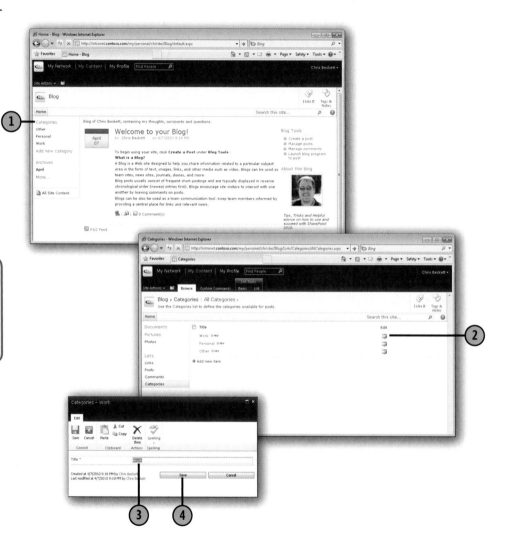

Managing Blog Posts

In the land of Blog, content is king! Creating blog posts allows you to promote your expertise, share information, and help your colleagues and coworkers stay up to date on your professional and personal activities. You can also edit blog posts you created previously to change or update the original content.

Create a Blog Post

(1) Click Create A Post on the Blog Tools menu.

(2) Enter values for your new post.

(3) Save your blog post by doing any of the following:

- Click Publish to save the post as ready for public display. Once the publishing date is reached, the post is automatically displayed on your site.

- Click Save As Draft to save your current version. The post will not be displayed to site visitors until you publish the post at a later time.

Publish a Blog Post Previously Saved as a Draft

① Click Manage Posts on the Blog Tools menu.

② Check one or more posts whose approval status indicates Pending.

③ Click the Items tab under List Tools on the ribbon.

④ Click Approve/Reject.

⑤ Select the Approved option in the dialog box that appears.

⑥ Click OK.

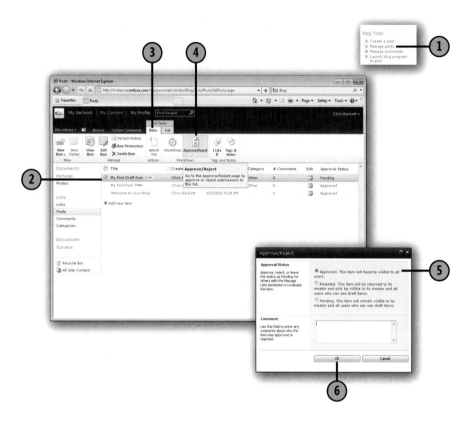

Managing Blog Comments

Comments allow blog sites to become collaboration tools. When a viewer adds a comment on a blog post, it creates a dialogue between the author, the person adding the comment, and other viewers, who can enhance and expand the original information.

Add a Comment

1. Click the Comments icon on the Social Tools menu.

2. Enter a title and body for your comment. (You may have to scroll down a bit to see the Add Comment section.)

3. Click Submit Comment.

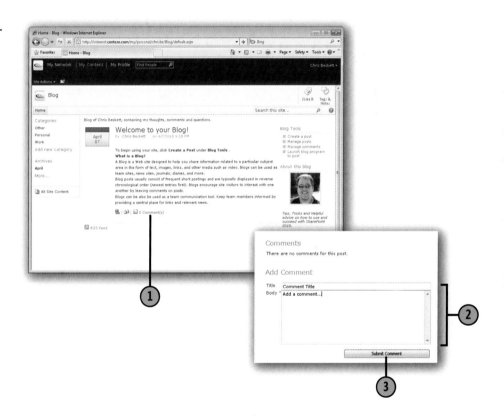

View, Edit, or Delete Comments

① Click Manage Comments on the Blog Tools menu.

② Select a comment row.

③ Click the Items tab under List Tools on the ribbon.

④ In the Manage group, click any of the following:

- Click View Item to view the comment details.

- Click Edit Item to edit the comment details.

- Click Delete Item to delete the command permanently.

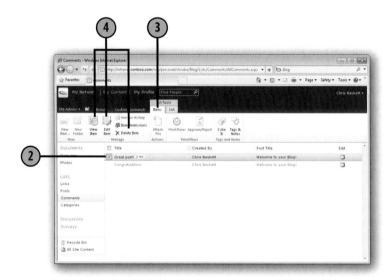

Subscribing to a Blog RSS Feed

Really Simple Syndication (RSS) is a standards protocol for streaming content updates over the Internet. It allows you to easily track new content being added to a favorite Web site or blog. SharePoint blog sites automatically enable an RSS feed for posts and comments for visitors.

A large number of RSS clients, called *feed readers,* can be used to subscribe to an RSS feed, including Internet Explorer 8 and Microsoft Outlook.

Subscribe to RSS

1. Click the RSS Feed link.

2. Click the Subscribe To This Feed link to open subscription options.

3. Click Subscribe to bookmark your feed subscription.

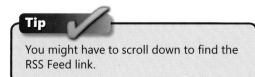

Tip

You might have to scroll down to find the RSS Feed link.

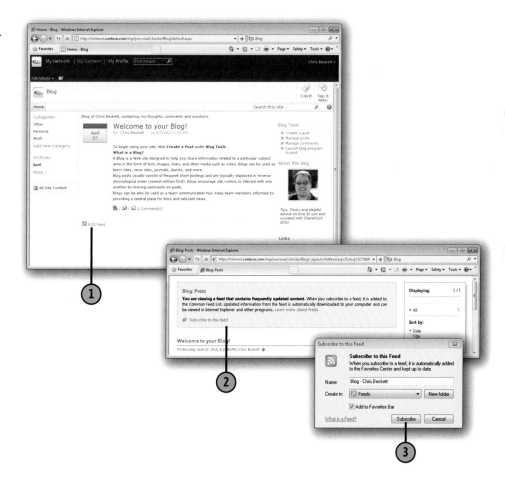

Using Desktop Blogging Tools to Publish Blog Posts

SharePoint blog sites support a Web service interface called the *MetaWeblog API* that enables desktop blogging tools that support it to publish posts to your blog. Both Microsoft Word and Windows Live Writer support publishing to a SharePoint blog.

The following list details some key advantages of using a desktop blogging tool.

- A richer user experience that is more responsive than a Web interface

- A larger working space for editing larger posts

- Richer tools for working with pictures and other objects you insert in your blog

Publish a Blog Post from Microsoft Word

① Click Launch Blog Program To Post on the Blog Tools menu.

② Click OK to register a new SharePoint blog account with the default settings.

(continued on next page)

Try This!

You can also open and edit existing posts in Microsoft Word. From the Blog Post tab on the ribbon, try opening an existing post, making a change, and then publishing the change back to your blog.

Publish a Blog Post from
Microsoft Word   *(continued)*

(3) Select the title field, and type your blog post title.

(4) Edit the body of your blog post.

(5) Click the Blog Post tab on the ribbon.

(6) Apply any formatting to your post using the Basic Text group or Quick Styles.

(7) Click Publish when you finish editing.

Try This!

Microsoft Word provides more options for inserting media into your blog, including clip art and SmartArt objects. Explore the Insert tab on the ribbon, and try inserting a piece of SmartArt in your blog post.

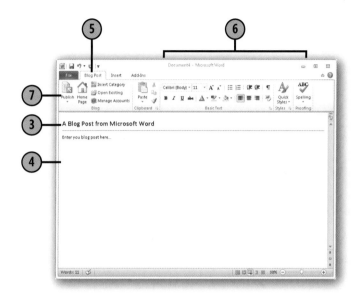

Security Within SharePoint 2010

Security for any organization is of vital importance. After all, an organization would not last long if it were unable to protect its content from unauthorized eyes.

Microsoft SharePoint 2010 comes equipped with robust security measures, so you can feel confident that your content is safe. The security model in SharePoint 2010 is very flexible as well, allowing security to be applied at the level of the farm, a web application, a site collection, sites, lists and libraries, or items.

It is beyond the scope of this book to describe the security measures above the level of a site collection. Therefore, this section illustrates how to set security for a site, lists and libraries, and individual items.

Understanding SharePoint Security

For anyone or anything to have access to content in SharePoint, they have to be granted permission to do so. This means that if you want to do anything within SharePoint, someone has to give you access first.

SharePoint 2010 allows permissions to be granted to groups of people or to individuals. In SharePoint 2010, SharePoint administrators can grant Active Directory groups access to the environment. This new functionality means that the groups you are a member of within your current Windows network can be used within SharePoint. However, the Active Directory groups still need to be given access to the individual elements within SharePoint.

Think of a group as a container of individuals. By working with groups, you are able to apply security settings to many individual users (up to five thousand) at one time. It's preferable to use groups for security within SharePoint rather than assign permissions directly to individuals.

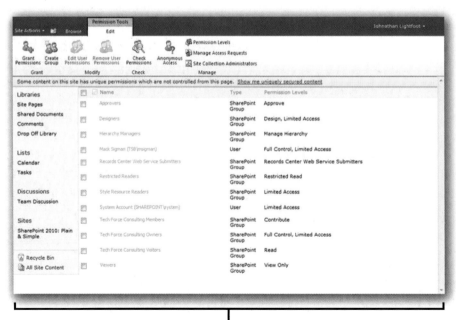

SharePoint administrators can grant
permissions to groups as well as individuals

Adding People to Groups

When a site is created, SharePoint automatically provides three security groups—the Visitors, Members, and Owners groups. Additional groups may be created depending on the type of site.

Remember that groups are only containers of users; groups need be given permissions to be of any use. You do this by applying a permission level to a group. A permission level is a set of rules (permissions) that determines what a group can do on a site, list, library, or item. When a team site is set up, SharePoint creates six permission levels:

- **Full Control**   Allows total control of a site. Users at this level can add, delete, approve, move, and create new sites.

- **Design**   Users at this level can view, add, delete, update, approve, and customize a SharePoint site.

- **Contribute**   Users at this level can view, add, update, and delete list items and documents.

- **Read**   Users at this level can view pages and list items and download documents.

- **Limited Access**   Users at this level can view specific lists and document libraries when given access.

- **View Only**   Similar to the Read permission level, but users at this level cannot download items.

Permission levels provide a set of rules known as individual permissions. Through individual permissions, an administrator is able to control what someone can or cannot do within SharePoint. SharePoint has a total of 33 individual permissions. Individual permissions can be mixed and matched in a variety ways to define literally thousands of permissions levels.

Once a site is created, the Visitors group is given Read permissions, the Members group is given Contribute permissions, and the Owners group is given Full Control permissions.

Note that SharePoint permissions are very comprehensive. For our purposes, we will work with permissions in My Site instead of the production SharePoint site. This allow us to show you how to work with permissions, but without affecting the production site collection.

Add People to Groups

① Click Site Permissions on the Site Actions menu.

② Click Grant Permissions on the Permission Tools Edit tab.

③ Under Select Users, type the person's name in the Users/Groups box and then press Enter, or click the Browse button and select a user.

④ Under Grant Permissions, use the drop-down list to select the group that you want to add the person to.

⑤ Click OK. (You might have to scroll down to see the button.)

Try This!

Add yourself to the Visitors group. Don't worry; you will not mess up your permissions by doing so.

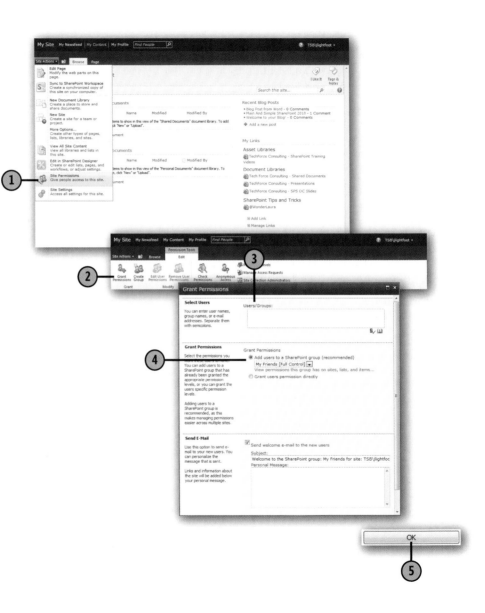

Creating Groups

The default groups are often not flexible enough for organizations to use. When this is the case, organizations can create their own groups to effectively grant access. SharePoint can support up to five thousand groups in each site collection, so you can set up groups to be as specific as you need them to be with regards to permissions. When setting up a new group, you have to name it, assign it a permission level, and add people to it.

Create a Group

① Click Site Permissions on the Site Actions menu.

② Click Create Group on the Permission Tools Edit tab.

③ Enter a name for the group.

④ Enter a description of the group.

⑤ Choose a permission level for the group.

⑥ Click OK.

Try This!

Create a group named Contractors. Which permission level do you think you would assign to the new group?

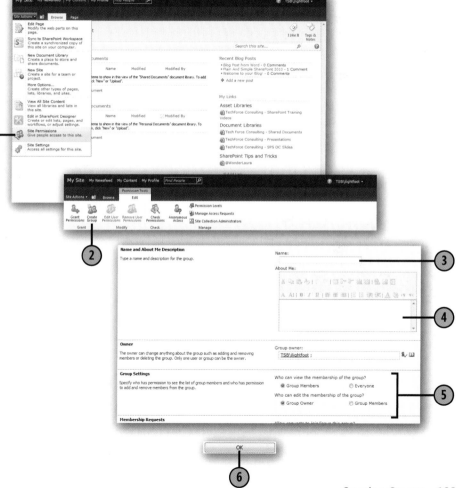

Granting Permissions to an Individual

It is generally considered a best practice to assign people to groups when granting permissions. By doing so you can easily see what permissions someone has, and you can then reproduce those results simply by adding someone to the same group. However, you might need to assign permissions to a user directly to grant access to a site or its individual elements. Assigning permissions to an individual is very similar to assigning a permission level to a group, but you make the assignment to a user profile instead.

Grant an Individual Permissions

① Click Site Permissions on the Site Actions menu.

② Click Grant Permissions on the Permission Tools Edit tab.

(continued on next page)

Grant an Individual
Permissions *(continued)*

③ Under Select Users, type the person's name or use the Browse button to select a user.

④ Under Grant Permissions, select the Grant Users Permission Directly option.

⑤ Select the permission level for the person.

⑥ Click OK.

Tip

Microsoft indicates that SharePoint groups can have up to five thousand members without adversely affecting performance. Imagine that you did not use groups, gave permissions directly to five thousand people, and then had to change all these permissions in one day. This is a perfect illustration of the benefits of using groups.

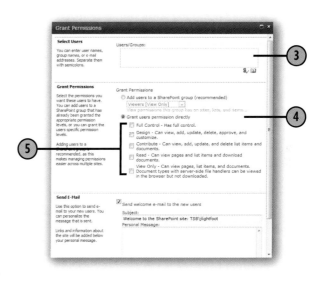

Breaking Inheritance

By default, child objects (sites, lists, and libraries) inherit their permissions from their parent object. As such, permissions for objects that are controlled by their parent object (and the permissions in effect for the parent) cascade to the child. For example, a site inherits the permissions of the parent site it was created under. A library, in turn, inherits the permissions of the site it is created in, and a document inherits the permissions of the library it is uploaded to. If an object inherits permissions, you need to stop inheritance before you can change the object's permissions.

Perhaps you have a list of contact information for everyone in your company. By default, everyone who has access to the list can see the information it contains. However, let's say that you need to restrict the list so that only users who are directors or above can see the contact information for senior executives. This is a situation in which you would break inheritance from the parent list and then apply permissions so that only members of your directors group could see the information.

Break Inheritance

① On the Quick Launch bar, select the list or library you want to work with.

(continued on next page)

Tip

If you re-inherit permissions from a parent object, any special permission levels that you set on the child object are deleted, and the permissions for the parent are the only ones in effect.

Tip

When you break inheritance, the object is on its own, so future changes to permissions on the parent site no longer cascade to the child item. You must apply future permission changes to the child object itself; SharePoint doesn't do it for you.

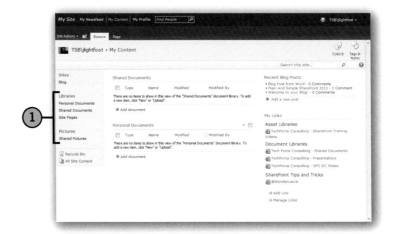

Break Inheritance *(continued)*

② Under Library Tools on the ribbon, click the Library tab.

③ In the Settings group, click Library Permissions.

④ Click Stop Inheriting Permissions on the Permission Tools Edit tab.

⑤ Click OK.

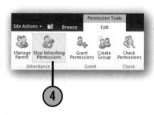

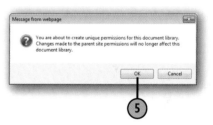

Tip

We recommend that you try to use inherited permissions whenever possible. The administrative load you encounter by breaking inheritance merits serious thought and discussion before you take this step.

Try This!

Stop inheriting permissions, and then start inheriting again.

Granting Access to Lists, Libraries, and Individual Items

SharePoint 2010 allows very granular application of security requirements. This means that you can apply security at the site collection level, the site level, the library or list level, and to individual items in a library or list.

For example, you might grant a group Member permissions to your site, but you might want to give the group only Read access to a certain library and only View Only access to a particular document in the library. With the flexible security model in SharePoint, you can make all these changes with no problem at all.

Grant Access to a List or Library

(1) On the Quick Launch bar, select the list or library you want to work with.

(2) Under Library Tools on the ribbon, select the Library tab.

(3) In the Settings group, click Library Permissions.

(continued on next page)

Grant Access to a List or Library *(continued)*

④ Click Grant Permissions on the Permission Tools Edit tab.

⑤ Type the person's name in the Users/Group box.

⑥ Specify whether to add the user to a group or to grant permissions directly.

⑦ Click OK.

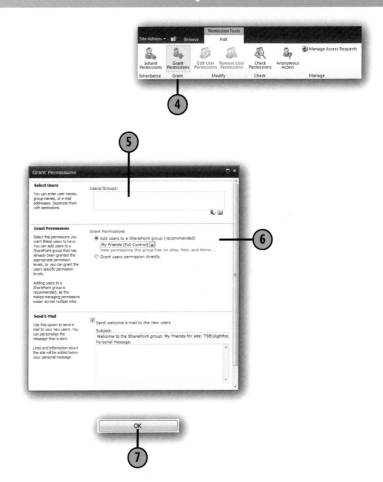

Grant Access to Individual Items

1. Click the down arrow for the item you want to give access to. You have to hover your mouse pointer over the item to see this arrow.

2. Click Manage Permissions.

3. Click Stop Inheriting Permissions on the Permission Tools Edit tab.

4. Click OK.

(continued on next page)

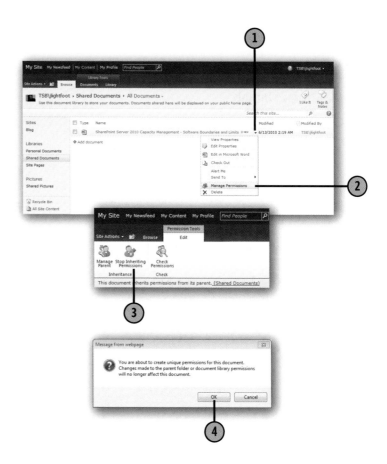

Grant Access to Individual

Items *(continued)*

⑤ Click Grant Permissions on the Permission Tools Edit tab.

⑥ Type the person's name in the Users/Groups box, or use the Browse button to select a user.

⑦ Select either the Add Users To A SharePoint Group or the Grant Users Permission Directly option.

⑧ If you are granting permissions directly, select the appropriate permission level.

⑨ Click OK.

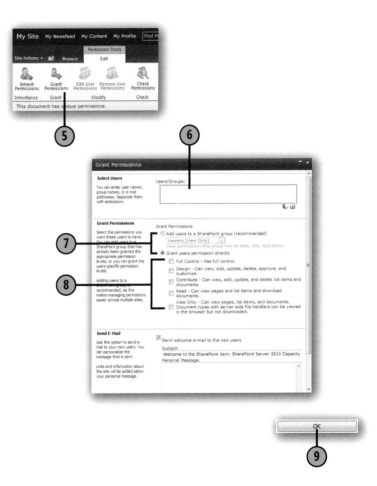

Removing Security

Naturally, if you are able to grant access, you are also able to remove it. SharePoint makes removing security very easy, because the steps required for granting access are the same for removing access. When you remove access, you can begin to see the power of groups.

Let's say you need to remove all permissions to your SharePoint site that were previously assigned to an individual. If you had not previously assigned this person to a group, and instead gave permissions directly to the user, you would have to locate every instance where you assigned individual permissions to remove them all. Additionally, if you consider the complexity that breaking inheritance to objects adds to your site, you can see that you would have a much harder time ensuring that access is completely removed for individually assigned permissions.

Remove Someone from a Group

1. Click Site Permissions on Site Actions menu.

2. Click the name of group you want to remove the person from.

(continued on next page)

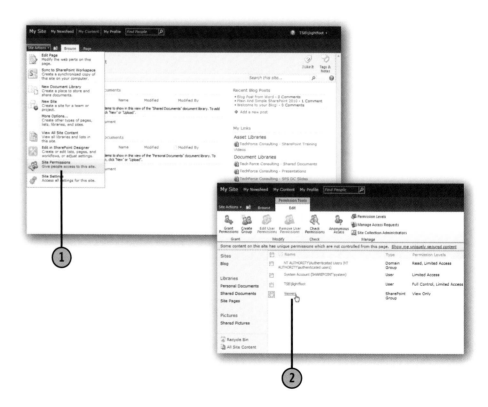

Remove Someone from a
Group *(continued)*

3 Select the check box next to the name of the person you want to remove.

4 Click Remove Users From Group on the Actions menu.

5 Click OK.

Remove a Group's Site Permissions

1. Click Site Permissions on the Site Actions menu.

2. Click the check box adjacent to the group you want to remove permissions from.

3. Select Remove User Permissions on the Permission Tools Edit tab.

4. Click OK.

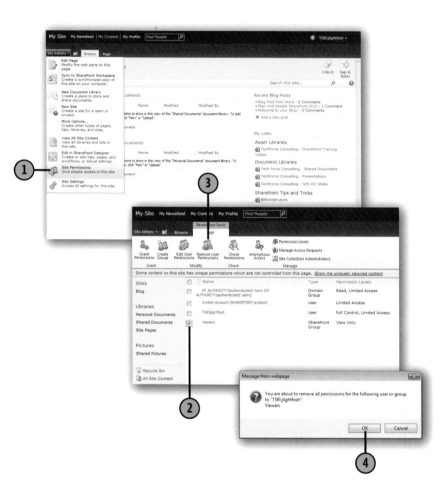

Checking Permissions

With the granular security capabilities that SharePoint provides, it is easy to lose track of who has access to your site, library, or item. Luckily, SharePoint provides you with the ability to check permissions that are applied to an object.

By using the ribbon, you can quickly find out what permissions are on an entire site, or you can query SharePoint to see what permissions a group or an individual has.

View Permissions on a Library

① Click All Site Content on the Quick Launch bar.

② Click the library you want to work with.

③ Click Library Permissions in the Settings group on the Library tab.

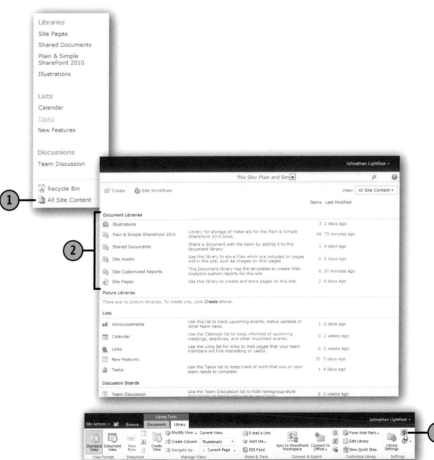

Check Permissions for a User

① Click Site Permissions on the Site Actions menu.

② Click Check Permissions in the Check group on the Permission Tools Edit tab.

③ Type the person's or group's name in the User/Group box.

④ Click Check Now.

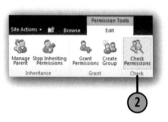

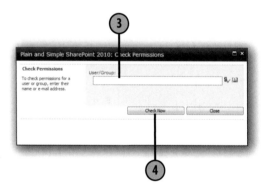

Using Personal Sites and Social Networking

You have probably used SharePoint to work with your team on projects. On those team sites, you can work in an open manner with members of your team to complete projects, but you don't have any place you can use to store content that you find of special interest. If your organization is running Microsoft SharePoint 2010 Enterprise Edition, you might have a feature called My Site available to you.

Simply stated, a My Site is your personal SharePoint 2010 Web site. On it you can list what your interests are and have SharePoint scour sites you have permissions for to present information you find of interest. You can also tag content you come across (within SharePoint or on external Web sites) and store it in your My Site.

Introducing My Site

With your interests entered on your My Site, someone looking for a person with your particular skill set can locate you rather easily. My Sites can also include a personal blog that you can use to document your observations about your daily work life. You are also able to invite colleagues to access and share your information as well.

My Site features include a My Networks page for managing colleagues, interests, and newsfeed settings; a My Content page for managing documents and photos; and a My Profile page for managing your user profile, social tags and notes, and similar information.

My Sites can be used in a number of ways:

- To share documents, lists, or blog content

- To identify documents, pages, and other information as potentially of interest to others you work with

- To update information about suggested keywords and colleagues that you have approved

- To store personal information such as contact information, interests, responsibilities, and e-mail list memberships

Open Your My Site

① Click My Site on the User menu.

Tip

Depending on your organization's governance plan, you might or might not have My Site functionality enabled. This functionality is available by default in an out-of-the-box installation.

Tip

You should check whether your organization has policies about sharing information. For example, your organization might have policies in place that determine what content can be stored online.

Editing Your User Profile

Have you ever worked for an organization and at times wished you had people with certain skills on hand to help you with a project? Or have you found out long after a project is complete (and outside help brought in at an additional cost) that your company had a guru familiar with the topic for which you needed expertise—she just happened to work in a department you don't normally interact with?

Through user profiles in My Sites, you have a powerful tool with which to locate people and potentially avoid these types of scenarios. While user profiles allow you to easily locate people that you need to interact or connect with, at the same time they let you showcase your skills and interests for others.

Perhaps you work in Accounting, but you are a secret "midnight programmer." In the past, you might not have been approached to assist with any programming projects. With My Sites, you can advertise your skills and interests, and should a need arise, you could be called upon.

One of the things you should do when you access your My Site for the first time is update your user profile. When SharePoint is deployed, the My Site functionality is not customized very much, meaning that your site might have only your user name and e-mail address listed. This level of detail is not very helpful when someone needs to find people with a certain expertise or people with certain interests.

Edit Your User Profile

1. Click My Profile.
2. Click Edit My Profile.
3. You can update your information in the following areas:
   - Basic Information
   - Contact Information
   - Details
   - Newsfeed Settings
4. Click Save and Close.

Tip

You have to be on your My Site to do this exercise.

Try This!

Update your user profile with your current information.

Uploading Content

Your My Site is set up with a few libraries by default, the two biggest being the Personal Documents and Shared Documents libraries. The Personal Documents library is used for documents that you do not want to share with other people. You might use this library when you need to access documents from multiple computers, but you don't want to share the documents with others. The Shared Documents library is used to store documents that you want to share with other people. Depending on the set up of your My Site, you might be able to edit the permissions for this library as well as for specific folders and items it contains.

On the Content tab of your user profile, people can view public documents that you create on other SharePoint sites you are a member of, as long as they have permission to view that content.

Upload Content to Your My Site Shared Documents

① Click My Content.

② Click Add Document in the Shared Documents Web Part.

③ Click Browse.

(continued on next page)

Upload Content to Your My Site
Shared Documents *(continued)*

④ Click the file that you want to upload.

⑤ Click Open.

⑥ Click OK.

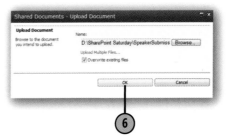

Upload Content to Your My Site Personal Documents

① Click My Content.

② Click Add Document in the Personal Documents Web Part.

③ Click Browse.

(continued on next page)

Upload Content to Your My Site
Personal Documents   *(continued)*

④ Click the file that you want to upload.

⑤ Click Open.

⑥ Click OK.

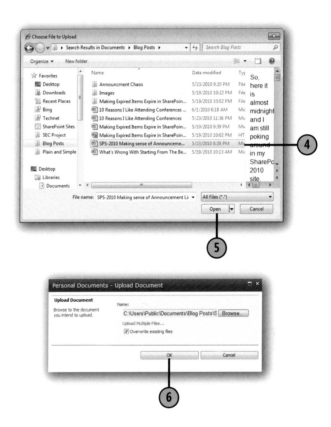

Tracking Colleagues

Chances are good that in your daily life you come across colleagues, coworkers, industry gurus, or other people who you share common interests with. Perhaps there is a person that has a lot of experience in your line of work and you enjoy reading their insights, discussions, or blog posts. With SharePoint Server 2010, you are able to keep up with these sources rather easily. By using your My Site, you can set up a central location for these sources that you can refer to anytime.

By the same token, you can be tracked by others. With this type of functionality, you are now able to collaborate in ways

that were unheard of a few short years ago. You can follow someone's postings, and if they happen to post something that you find of interest, you can tag it for later reference or perhaps use the information immediately to assist you with your project.

In this section, we go over how to add a colleague, edit information about colleagues, and remove colleagues from your My Site.

Add a Colleague

① Click My Colleagues.

(continued on next page)

Tip

If you are not sure of the spelling of your colleague's name, you can always use the Browse button and then type the portion of the name you are sure about to get a list of suggestions.

Add a Colleague *(continued)*

② Click Add Colleagues.

③ Type your colleague's name or user name for SharePoint, and then press Enter.

④ Specify whether this person is on your team.

⑤ Specify the group you want to add the colleague to.

⑥ Click OK.

Try This!

Add a few of your coworkers to your Colleagues list.

Edit Colleague Information

① Click My Colleagues.

② Select the check box next to the colleague you want to edit.

③ Click Edit Colleagues.

④ Specify whether this person is on your team.

⑤ Specify the group you want to add the colleague to.

⑥ Click OK.

Tip

Did you notice that you are not actually editing information about the colleague? You are merely changing the group the colleague belongs to. Only your colleagues can change their attributes.

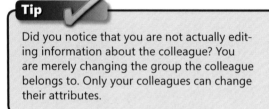

Remove a Colleague

① Click My Colleagues.

② Select the check box next to the colleague that you want to remove.

③ Click Remove Colleagues.

④ Click OK.

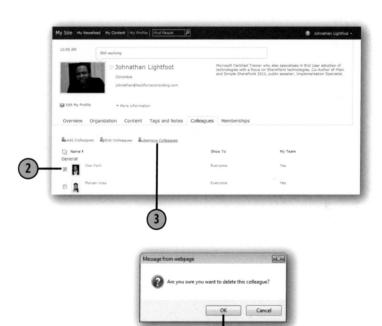

Updating Your Status

Chances are that you use social networking sites such as Twitter, Facebook, LinkedIn, or Flickr. Each of these sites has an area where you can post what you are doing or your status. Adding this information allows you to keep your family or friends abreast of your activities. Initially, the status information that was posted was comical and sometimes downright useless. As such, people sometimes shied away from posting their status. After all, do people really care how many beers someone is drinking on a Saturday night?

The fine developers at Microsoft started thinking that SharePoint could also be used as a social networking platform for the business enterprise. So, with SharePoint 2010, you can post information about what you are doing. Because you will most likely use SharePoint 2010 in a business context, you won't post personal status messages (such as "Heading out to the pub to tie one on"); you will instead want to post that you are in a meeting, researching a certain topic, or trying to connect with a certain group of people possessing a certain skill set. By doing so you enable your colleagues to assist you with whatever task is at hand, while at the same time you let people know what you are working on.

Update Your Status

1. Click My Profile.

2. Click in the notification balloon in which your status is displayed.

3. Highlight the text, enter your updated status text, and then press Enter.

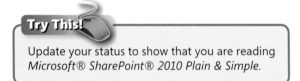

Update your status to show that you are reading *Microsoft® SharePoint® 2010 Plain & Simple*.

View Colleague Status

① Click My Site.

Tip

Did you notice that, merely by going to your My Site, you are presented with a status report for your colleagues?

Using Your Note Board

In your daily life you often come across content that you find especially helpful or useful. In the past, when you were online and came across an article you thought was useful, you might have saved the link to your favorites. With SharePoint 2010, you can now do the same thing, with the added benefit of adding a note or comment about the content. Perhaps you liked an article because of the way it approached the technical side of a subject. If that's the case, you can make a note on your Note Board so that your colleagues know not only that you liked the article but why you liked it.

Previously, when you marked content as a favorite item, you often ended up with hundreds of favorites, and after a few months you could not tell why you selected a certain item to be a favorite. With the Note Board feature, this problem becomes a thing of the past.

With the Add SharePoint Tags And Notes tool, the SharePoint Server 2010 Note Board feature even works outside SharePoint while you are browsing the Web.

Create a Note on Content Within SharePoint

(1) On the Quick Launch bar, click the list or library that contains the content you want to work with.

(continued on next page)

Create a Note on Content Within SharePoint *(continued)*

2 Select the check box next to the document you want to make a note about. You have to hover over the item's name to see the check box.

3 Click Tags & Notes in the Tags And Notes group on the Documents tab.

4 Click the Note Board tab.

5 Type your note.

6 Click Post.

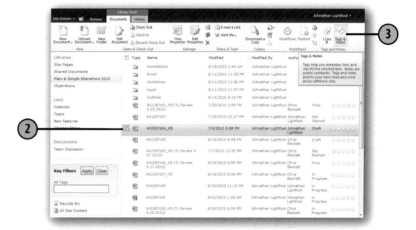

Add the SharePoint Tags And Notes Tool to Your Favorites

① Click My Site on the User menu.

② Click My Profile.

③ Click Tags And Notes.

④ Right-click the link that reads "Right click or drag and drop this link to your browser's favorites or bookmarks toolbar to tag external sites."

⑤ Click Add To Favorites.

⑥ Click Yes.

⑦ Click Add.

Try This!

Add the SharePoint Tags And Notes tool to your favorites.

Tip

These instructions are for Internet Explorer 8. The steps might be different on other browsers.

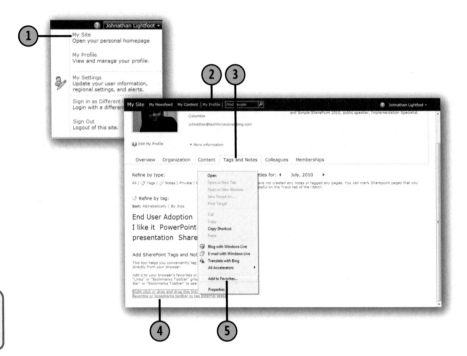

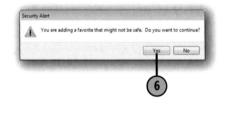

Add a Note to Content on an External Site

① Click Favorites.

② Click Tags And Note Board.

③ Click the Note Board tab.

④ Type your note.

⑤ Click Post.

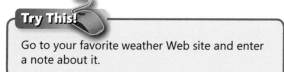

Tip

This exercise uses an external site, not a SharePoint site.

Try This!

Go to your favorite weather Web site and enter a note about it.

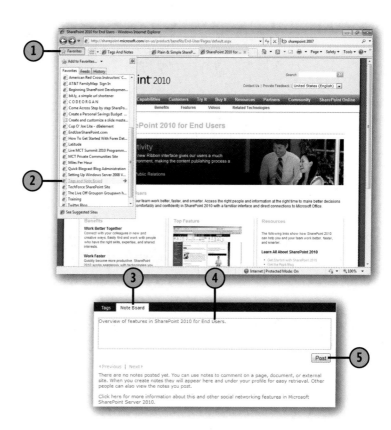

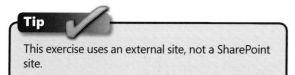

View Notes

① Click My Site on the User menu.

② Click My Profile.

③ Click Tags And Notes.

④ View the notes under the Activities For section.

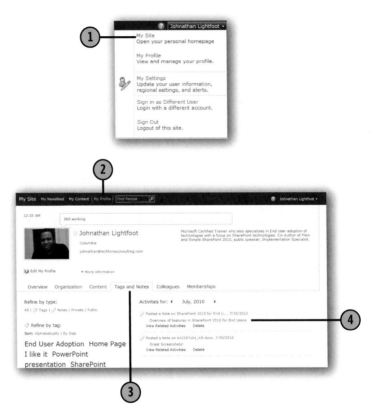

14

Searching for Information

Almost from the beginning, Microsoft recognized the need for a rich search engine within the SharePoint platform. In early versions, Microsoft delivered comprehensive search solutions, and while these worked well for most people, Microsoft continued to improve the features.

As more and more content is produced, it becomes imperative that we be able to find the information we need in a timely manner. It is also important that we are able to find people as well as content. Within your organization you might have official titles that are attached to or associated with a certain department, division, or unit. But what about the skills you have that are not directly related to your official title? How can someone discover those?

Microsoft SharePoint 2010 allows you to conduct searches for content or people through a very easy interface that assures you that you are receiving the information you need.

Introducing Search Center

You are probably familiar with the built-in search box that appears in the title section of your SharePoint site. Although the search box is a powerful feature for searching for content, sometimes you might need an even more powerful search component.

SharePoint Server 2010 includes a feature called the Search Center. The Search Center is a site that is specifically dedicated to searching. There are three types of Search Centers that you can create in SharePoint 2010:

- **Enterprise Search Center**   Has a Welcome page that includes a search box with two tabs: one for general searches (documents, spreadsheets, and so on), and another for searching for information about people. You can add and customize tabs to focus on other search scopes or result types.

- **Basic Search Center**   This site includes pages for search results and advanced searches.

- **FAST Search Center**   A site for delivering the FAST search experience. The Welcome page includes a search box with two tabs: one for general searches, and another for searches for information about people. You can add and customize tabs to focus on other search scopes or result types.

You can also customize the Search Center by using Web Parts. When a Search Center is created, numerous Web Parts are set up that you can add to your Search Center or to your team site. With these Web Parts, you can perform searches from anywhere within SharePoint.

Maybe your team searches on a certain term, such as "budget." When this search occurs, you know that the majority of the time team members are looking for the current fiscal year budget spreadsheet. To facilitate this need, you can set up something known as a best bet. A best bet is a predefined result that you can configure so that when someone enters the keywords you designate, they see the best bet result at the top of the search results, thus saving the user lots of time looking for relevant information.

Also, in the past you might have performed a search and received hundreds of results; a new feature called refiners addresses this problem with searching in SharePoint. Refiners appear listed on the left side of the search results and are based on tags, categories, and other metadata. You can click a refiner to narrow the results you see.

For example, perhaps you searched on the phrase "2010 budget" and received more than 500 results. You could use a refiner to look only for Word documents authored by a particular person. By using refiners, you can get to the content that you are looking for more quickly.

> **Tip** ✓
>
> FAST is a recursive acronym for Fast Search and Transfer ASA, which is the name of a Norwegian company that Microsoft acquired in April 2008. The search technology the company developed is now an add-on to SharePoint, and it provides a very rich search experience. If you want to learn more about FAST search within SharePoint, you can go to *http://sharepoint.microsoft.com/en-us/product/capabilities/search/Pages/Fast-Search.aspx.*

Create a Search Center

(1) Click New Site on the Site Actions menu.

(2) Click Search in the Filter By list.

(3) Click the type of Search Center you want to create. (Depending on your setup, not all Search Centers may be available to you.)

(4) Type a title for the Search Center.

(5) Type the URL for the Search Center.

(6) Click Create.

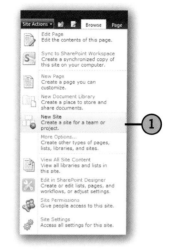

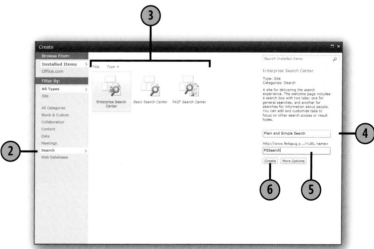

Access a Search Center

① Click All Site Content on the Quick Launch bar.

② Click the name of your Search Center, located in the Sites And Workspaces section. (You might have to scroll down to see the Search Center name.)

Perform a Search with Search Center

① In the search box, enter the keyword(s) you are looking for.

② Click the magnifying glass icon.

Tip

To perform this operation, you need access to your Search Center. For instructions on accessing a Search Center, see "Access a Search Center" above.

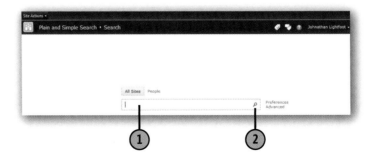

Using Search Scopes

The Search Center is designed to be completely customizable. For example, you can create scopes, which are rules that determine from where you want your search results returned. Perhaps you are looking for documents located on a specific SharePoint site. You can set up a scope to return results only from that site. There are four types of scope rules that you can set up:

- **All Content**   Includes all content that is available in a content index.

- **Content Source**   Gives you the ability to limit the scope to a specific content source; for example, a file share or a database.

- **Property Query**   Lets you build a scope based on managed properties such as File Extension. For example, you can build a scope that returns only .xlsx files. Now, instead of the results including Word documents or PowerPoint presentations, you receive only Excel spreadsheets.

- **Web Address**   Enables you to build a scope targeting a specific site, list, or folder in a library.

Setting up a search scope is a two part process. The first step is to create the scope, which includes giving it a title and description and determining what group you want to associate it with.

The second step in creating a scope is to define its rules. The rules tell the scope what it is or is not looking for. It is in this step that you select the scope rule type, along with setting the query information. The scope rule type you select determines the query information that you need to add. If you select Web Address as the scope rule type, you are asked to enter the Web address for the folder, hostname, or domain (or subdomain). Alternatively, if you select the Property Query scope rule type, you have to enter the property restriction information.

Finally, you need to select how you want to apply the scope (also known as its behavior). You have three choices:

- **Include**   Any item that matches the rule is included, unless the item is excluded by another rule.

- **Require**   Every item in the scope must match this rule.

- **Exclude**   Items matching this rule are excluded from the scope.

Tip

By default you have two groups: Search Dropdown and Advanced Search. These correspond with the default search options in SharePoint 2010. If your site collection administrator chooses to, he or she can add custom groups.

Tip

If you select the All Content scope rule type, you aren't asked for any additional information. SharePoint automatically searches all content to return results for you.

Create a Search Scope

① Click Site Settings on the Site Actions menu.

② Click Go To Top Level Site Settings in the Site Collection Administration Group.

③ Click Search Scopes in the Site Collection Administration Group.

(continued on next page)

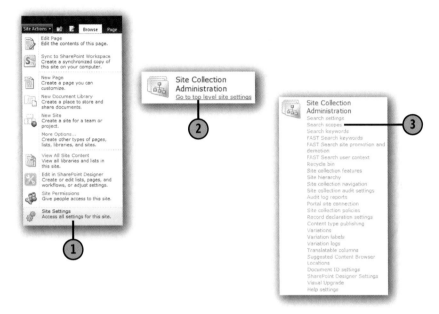

Create a Search Scope *(continued)*

4 Click New Scope.

5 Enter a title and a description for the scope.

6 Select which scope groups you want to include the scope in.

7 Click OK.

Add Rules to a Search Scope

1. Click Site Settings on the Site Actions menu.

2. Click Go To Top Level Site Settings in the Site Collection Administration Group.

3. Click Search Scopes in the Site Collection Administration Group.

4. Click the scope you want to add rules to.

5. Click New Rule in the Rules section.

6. Select the scope rule type.

7. Fill in the query type section. (If you select the All Content scope rule type, you can skip this step.)

8. Select the behavior.

9. Click OK.

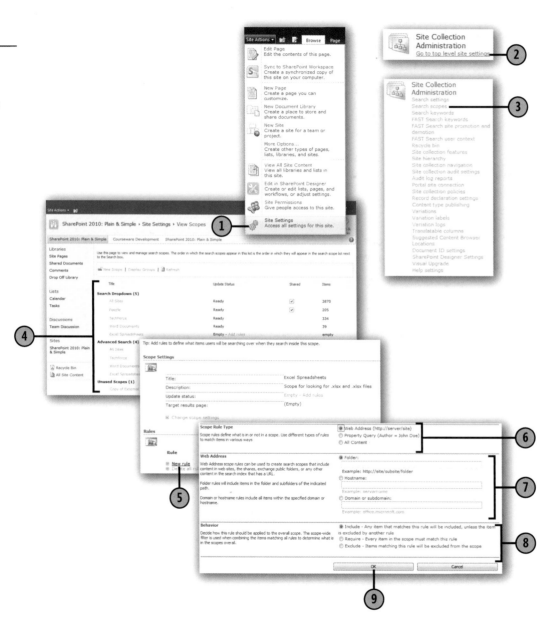

Using Refiners

If you have used Bing, Google, or any other search engine, you may have received far more results than you were expecting. Searching in SharePoint 2010, you could end up with the same experience. A new feature in SharePoint 2010 is the use of refiners. Refiners are rules based on the metadata defined in your content.

For example, you might search by using the keyword "policies" and receive hundreds of responses. Let's say that you

want results only for a particular author. In the list of refiners that appears in a task pane on the left side of your screen, you could go to the Author section and select the name of the author that you want to see in detail. If there are still a lot of results, you could use additional refiners to really drill down into the results to find exactly what you are looking for as quickly as possible.

Use Refiners

① Select the search scope you want to use from the drop-down list.

② Type your search term.

③ Click the magnifying glass icon.

④ Click the refiner you want to use.

Setting Up Best Bet Results

Maybe your team often searches using a term such as "budget." You know that the majority of the time team members are looking for the current fiscal year budget spreadsheet. You can set up something known as a best bet to help your team find this information. A best bet is a predefined result that you can configure so that when someone enters the keywords you designate, the user sees the best bet result at the top of the search results, thus saving the user lots of time looking for relevant information.

Setting up a best bet is a two part process. The first step consists of creating the keyword that you expect someone will search for. The second step is associating the best bet with the keyword. The best bet is the URL for the Web address that has the content you want to display in the results.

Create a Best Bet

① Click Site Settings on the Site Actions menu.

② Click Go To Top Level Site Settings in the Site Collection Administration section.

③ Click Search Keywords in the Site Collection Administration section.

④ Click Add Keyword.

(continued on next page)

Create a Best Bet   *(continued)*

⑤ Type your keyword in the Keyword Phrase box.

⑥ Click Add Best Bet.

⑦ Enter the URL for the content you want to display in the results.

⑧ Enter a title for the content.

⑨ Click OK.

⑩ Click OK again. (You might have to scroll down to see the OK button.)

Tip ✔

To get the URL for the content, navigate to the library that has the content, right-click the name of the file, and then select the Properties option. You can then copy the URL.

Subscribing to Search Results as an RSS Feed

You may have a certain topic or subject of interest that you like to stay abreast of. For example, perhaps you want to follow content related to a certain search that you set up. Instead of having to run the search regularly yourself, you can have SharePoint run the search for you and report any changes in the results. With SharePoint 2010 Server, you can now subscribe to search results as an RSS feed.

An RSS (Really Simple Syndication) feed provides you with a way to keep up on frequently updated content. Normally, people go to a Web site or a discussion board to view updated content. Some days there may be a lot of updates, and on other days there may be next to no updates. By subscribing to the site's RSS feed, you can get regular updates via Internet Explorer or another RSS reader program.

SharePoint uses this same concept, but instead of being limited to a single Web page or site, you can set up an RSS search that returns any content that has changed based on criteria that you choose. Once the search is set up, you don't have to run the same search regularly to catch any changes—the search runs automatically and informs you of any updated content.

Subscribe to Search Results as an RSS Feed

1. Run a search. (For instructions on running a search see "Perform a Search with Search Center" on page 218.)

(continued on next page)

Subscribe to Search Results as an RSS Feed *(continued)*

② Select any appropriate refiners. (For instructions for using refiners, see "Use Refiners" on page 223.)

③ Click the RSS icon.

④ Click Subscribe To This Feed.

⑤ Type a name for the feed.

⑥ Select the folder in which to create the feed.

⑦ Click Subscribe.

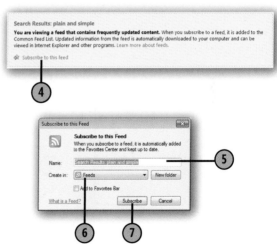

View Search Feeds in Internet Explorer 8

① Click Favorites.

② Click the Feeds tab.

③ Select the search feed you want to view.

View Search Feed in Outlook 2010

① Click RSS Feeds.

② Click the name of your SharePoint search feed.

Tip ✓

If do not see your search RSS feed listed, click File, Options, Advanced. In the RSS Feeds section, be sure that the check box is selected next to Synchronize RSS Feeds To The Common Feed List (CFL) Within Windows.

Tip ✓

Depending on the settings on your computer and your network, it might take a short time before the feed is updated in Outlook 2010.

Using Advanced Search

Depending on the amount of content on your network and what you are looking for, you might need more granular control over your results. By utilizing the advanced search features in SharePoint 2010, you can really zero in on the results you are looking for.

Advanced search features allow you to find documents that have:

- All of the words you specify.

- The exact phrase you specify.

- Any of the words you specify.

- None of the words you specify.

Use Advanced Search

1. Click Advanced.

2. Type the criteria for the content you are looking for.

3. Click Search.

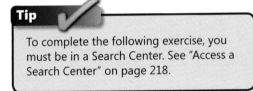

Tip

To complete the following exercise, you must be in a Search Center. See "Access a Search Center" on page 218.

You can also limit your results to certain languages. Out of the box, these languages include English, French, German, Japanese, Simplified Chinese, Spanish, and Traditional Chinese.

Perhaps you are looking for specific types of documents, such as Word, PowerPoint, or Excel files. By using Advanced Search, you can specify this. And finally, you can set up AND or OR criteria according to property information. For example, perhaps you want to locate documents authored by Johnathan Lightfoot and modified a week ago.

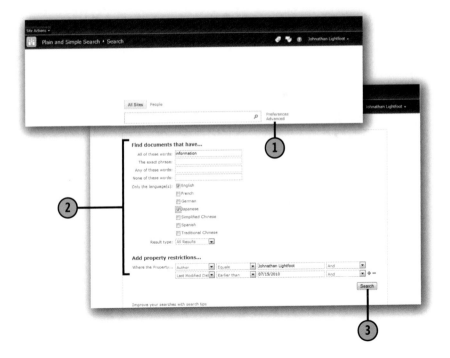

Index

A

B

C

N

O

About the Authors

Johnathan Lightfoot is the President/CEO of TechForce, Inc., a Microsoft partner company, and has been involved with IT for over 20 years. He has worked in various roles, including Help Desk, Level II and III Desktop Support, and Windows and AS-400 Server Administration and Development. Companies he is fortunate to have worked for in the past include Electronic Data Systems, Hawaiian Telcom, and Norwegian Cruise Line (yes, he actually worked on the ships). However, the best experiences he has had were during his nine years serving in the United States Navy.

Johnathan is a Microsoft Certified Trainer (MCT) who specializes in SharePoint 2010, MOSS 2007, WSS 3.0, and Office 2007 and 2010 technologies, along with providing soft skills training for organizations. Due to his background, he is often called upon by federal and state agencies during the rollout phase of SharePoint deployments to provide training (beginner, intermediate, and advanced) and to assist end users, power users, and site administrators with user acceptance, as well as to serve as the translator between end users and IT departments. He is certified as an MCT, MCDST, MCAS 2007, and MCPS (Microsoft Online Services).

Johnathan is from Miami, Florida, originally, but grew up in Mesquite, Texas; he has lived and worked literally around the world. He currently lives in Columbia, Maryland, with his super-terrific wife, Genevievette, and daughter, Giavrielle.

Chris Beckett is a Microsoft Certified SharePoint Master, with 20 years of business solutions expertise; six years of dedicated SharePoint solutions consulting experience; thousands of hours of knowledge acquisition, training, and professional development; and a deep expertise with SharePoint technologies. He is an active SharePoint community participant and writes a SharePoint-focused blog. He is also a frequent speaker at user group and industry events.

What do you think of this book?

We want to hear from you!

To participate in a brief online survey, please visit:

microsoft.com/learning/booksurvey

Tell us how well this book meets your needs—what works effectively, and what we can do better. Your feedback will help us continually improve our books and learning resources for you.

Thank you in advance for your input!

Stay in touch!